Papa Was a Rolling Stone

A Daughter's Journey To Forgiveness

Robin Wright King

ISBN: 0-9760755-4-7
       978-0-9760755-4-7

Library of Congress Control Number: 2007920075

Photograph by Marcus Hunter
Cover design by Ryan Brown

Author's website: www.robinwrightking.com

Published by:

Read4Life Books
An imprint of Christian Book Outreach, Inc.
P.O. Box 5145 Coralville Iowa 52241

T/Fax: 1-3193519695

Printed in Canada

BK58677

Praise for *Papa Was A Rolling Stone*

In *Papa Was A Rolling Stone: A Daughter's Journey to Forgiveness*, Robin Wright King forces our community to recognize and act on a situation that has permeated every level of our society. The life story of Wright King as chronicled in the book makes a compelling case for parents and everybody concerned about the future of our younger generation to work to prevent fatherlessness or motherlessness. This book strikes in the heart of a problem that demands our collective response as African Americans because the family has always been central to our community and in upholding our values. I commend Wright-King for urging everyone to act now.

— George W.B. Haley, Former U.S. Ambassador and brother of Roots author Alex Haley

Papa Was a Rolling Stone: A Daughter's Journey to Forgiveness is a profoundly moving, strikingly passionate, and inspired articulation of what it means to grow up without the nurturing presence of a loving father. It wakes us up to the enormity of the challenge facing all African American fathers: that our love and support for our daughters is fundamentally incalculable. Robin Wright King poignantly reminds us of the pain that is generated when fathers are absent and invisible, and she does so in a manner that is suffused with a unique blend of elegance, wisdom, and grace.

— Oliver J. Johnson, PhD., author of "Breaking the Chains Of Cocaine: Black Male Addiction and Recovery"

Papa Was A Rolling Stone: A Daughter's Journey To Forgiveness is one of most comprehensive and sociological reports on the absent father in Black families. Mrs. King combines a personal experience to a malignant paradigm with solutions to breaking this insidious situation within the Black community. Moreover, combining statistics with human experiences and bringing facts and numbers in our faces create and present a most obvious question, "What are we going to do now?" Papa Was a Rolling Stone will draw you in with love, educate you with facts, and motivate you to action and or advocacy with its answers.

— **Howard W. Starks Jr., Ed. Spec., Department of Africana Studies, Wayne State University, Detroit, MI**

Robin Wright King comes forth with great emotional depth, a stunningly vivid account of a parental void that should resonate with readers across a spectrum of experiences. The unique nature of the 'Father-Daughter' relationship is examined in all its beauty and frustration. This is a must-read for all daughters seeking to understand themselves in the context of a father lost."

— *Lee E. Meadows, PhD, Professor of Management at Walsh College, author of the Lincoln Keller Mystery series and* **Take the Lull by the Horns: A Business Fable.**

Papa Was A Rolling Stone: A Daughter's Journey to Forgiveness is a strong and moving account of one of our most pressing issues in America today: Fatherlessness. The life of Author Robin Wright King chronicled in this book is a vivid triumph of the human spirit and the power of struggle. If you are not ready to deal with or change your own difficult life situation, don't bother to pick up this book.

— *Bankole Thompson, editor of the **Michigan Chronicle** and author of "Ignoring The Underprivileged"*

Robin Wright King has chronicled a personal account of a father's failure to provide for his family and a daughter's deliverance from the disappointing and debilitating effects of that failure. The author spins a personal story the threads of which weave their way through her emotional foundations as a child and continued to adulthood. Robin's writing style engages the reader at both the feeling and thinking levels. The author draws the reader vicariously into her experience with such skill that you cannot read without reaction. The reader will want to say or do something to make a difference. Papa Was A Rolling Stone is a must read for all persons concerned with the pain and problems of the African American Family created by the attitude of absence and physical abandonment practiced by too many African American men.

—*Samuel H. Bullock, Jr., D. Min., Pastor of Bethany Baptist Church, President of the Council of Baptist Pastors of Detroit and Vicinity*

Papa Was a Rolling Stone

A DAUGHTER'S JOURNEY TO FORGIVENESS

PAPA WAS A ROLLING STONE
A DAUGHTER'S JOURNEY TO FORGIVENESS

Robin Wright King

"Biology is the very least of what is required to be a father."
Robin Wright King

My dear husband **Rev. Dr. Oscar King**, and

the two absolute joys of my life,

my sons

Roderick (Ricky) L Brown, II

Ryan B. Brown

who will grow to be strong and purposeful men and
perhaps experience the joy of fatherhood,

my late mother

Luvenia O. Lloyd Johnson

and

my late Gammy

Mary Eunice (Isabel) Lloyd

ACKNOWLEDGMENTS

It has taken six long years to bring this project to fruition. At the onset, it was easy to fill the pages with my thoughts. My emotions were high and the words were simply flying on to the paper. As the project matured, however, it became clear that just putting the words on paper was only half the battle. I found myself in several long reflective stages that resulted in my journey to forgiveness and personal recovery. I did not start this project with forgiveness in mind, but found it in the process. I did not start this journey knowing that I would find and develop wonderful new friends and the opportunity to enhance existing relationships. I could not have completed this journey without the encourage-ment, loyalty, and support from my family and friends and a wonderful team of professionals.

My mother, Luvenia O. Lloyd Johnson, is responsible for all that I am. She left her physical body on September 15, 1990, succumbing to breast cancer, but will be with me always. My grandmother, Mary Eunice Lloyd, provided me with a warm and loving hand that I will cherish forever. My stepfather, Kenneth Kendrick, is always there for me and is a shining example of a man. My mother's sister, Aunt Pat (Hadley), shared with me her insight to my mother's life and details that I would have otherwise not known. My aunt, Gloria, shared her memories of my mother's life as a young mother, describing her commitment and dedication to making a good life for her children. Gloria Matthews-Condelee and Shirley Allen, my mother's childhood friends, spent time with me to talk about the early days of my parents' relationship and provided significant insight to their lives. To my half-sister, Trina, thank you for your insight and your pleasant memories of our father. To my stepmother, Helen, I thank you for sharing the pictures of my father because the only picture I had prior to this book was the picture on his obituary.

I want to thank 'my girls,' Joan Thomas Knasiak and Gwen (Penny) Shannon, because you have been my rock and second voice for this book. Your friendship, support and 'sister love' are greatly appreciated. To Denise Dunn Roberts, my friend and agent, a special thanks for your support and tenacious advocacy for this book and for me.

I owe special thanks to my friend Debbie Schussel, a dynamite political analyst, lawyer and writer for the 'push' to write this book. Debbie encouraged me to stop talking about it and to start writing about it. To my 'native' son from the Gambia, Bankole Thompson, I thank you for your thoughtful ideas and your encouragement. You truly inspire me.

To my husband, Oscar King, thank you for your support and your living example of fatherhood to your children, Nicole and Oscar and their children, Khari and Bailey. I sincerely appreciate your love and support.

To my sister, Debra Alexandra Wright-Cross, I thank you sincerely for reviewing the book for accuracy, as our memories can get a little foggy with time. I thank you for being such a wonderful and loving sister and wish that everyone could have a sister like you. To my brother, Marcus Hunter, I thank you for the opportunity to witness fatherhood to my nieces Lauren and Madison. Their lives are better because of you.

To Tracey, Kenyatta, Kristen, Craig, Jennifer, Charlie II (posthumously), Charlie III (posthumously), and Cecelia, I love you.

To my sons' father and my former husband, Roderick L. Brown, I thank you for being the paradigm of a great father. It is my hope that when our sons, Ricky and Ryan, decide to become fathers, they will conduct their lives as 'father' by your example.

Finally, to the two most wonderful people in my world, my sons, Roderick (Ricky) L. Brown, II and Ryan B. Brown, I cannot imagine my life without you. I love you both dearly and I am honored to be your mother. You have taught me patience, compassion, the meaning of prayer, unconditional love, and positioned me for the most acclaimed role of my life, Mother.

Papa Was a Rolling Stone

A DAUGHTER'S JOURNEY TO FORGIVENESS

TABLE OF CONTENTS

Foreword

    As I begin the foreword to this book, I am reminded of the relationship I had with my own father. Although I only knew him for a brief period because he died when I was twelve-years old, my memory of him is that of a man who loved his wife, sacrificed for his family, and was always there for me. I thank God that I grew up knowing that men – particularly African-American men - had the potential to be good fathers. Although brief, I cannot imagine my life as a young boy without my father. I cannot imagine how difficult it is for children to grow up without their fathers.

    Robin Wright King's book, *Papa Was a Rolling Stone: A Daughter's Journey to Forgiveness*, is a powerfully written account of a daughter's life without her father. To her credit and catharsis, the book reads like a love letter from a loving daughter to her father who did not play an active role in her life. Unfortunately, it is a book about many contemporary African-American families wherein seven of every ten children are born out of wedlock and raised by single mothers. Robin Wright King speaks in a clear, yet emotional voice regarding the impact of father absence and meticulously chronicles high and low points that often left her confused, yet hopeful of his favor.

The book illuminates what I consider the "birth right of children" that is, to have two loving parents actively engaged and present in their lives. As she so eloquently points out, "we don't choose our parents." However, the magnitude of this responsibility is undeniable. Our children should experience and learn responsible parenting behaviors in our homes. Too often, they do not see responsible parent and adult images modeled in the home. They are left to figure it out, learning from the streets and the media what parenting is all about. Left to these devices, the result is often early promiscuity and young parents who are neither psychologically nor emotionally ready to assume this awesome duty that God has put before them.

Despite not having her father in her life, Robin Wright King's book is a story of resilience and courage. Thank God for loving mothers, grandmothers, and extended family members who serve as surrogates when fathers are absent in families. Robin has not only survived, but she has thrived in her role as a mother, and in her career.

More profoundly than any other aspect of this book, Robin

Wright King conveys the unconditional love of children toward their parents, "warts and all". She moves beautifully toward a path of forgiveness that allows her to heal and move on with life. She is blessed to have this capacity and provides an important road map for other daughters of absent fathers.

Finally, this book is a must-read for both men and women, but especially daughters of absent fathers. It will give you a sense of hope and inspiration and provide you with the tools to make the right choices about the men who father your children. Fathers play a vital role in the life of children and this book powerfully illustrates this fact.

Dr. Jeffery M. Johnson, author of several publications including *Fatherhood Development: A Curriculum for Young Fathers,* and President and CEO of the Washington DC-based nonprofit, National Partnership for Community Leadership (NPCL), has overseen the planning and implementation of two of the nation's largest social welfare research projects involving low-income men.

PREFACE

This is my story. This is the story of my life growing up without my father, the impact on my life and my path to recovery and forgiveness. *This is not a story about my father.* Writing this book has taken a tremendous amount of courage on several levels. First, I have known for years that the desire and the need to write this book have been there. I tucked away episode after episode of low grade but painful events related to the willful absence of my father to participate in my life. As a child, I was keenly aware of his absence but did not fully understand it. As I moved into adulthood, I dismissed him as irresponsible and worthless as I began to understand the concepts of character, ethics, and accountability. I began to comprehend the task my mother had taken on and the daunting and overwhelming place in which she found herself, barely twenty years old and raising two young girls, 355 days apart without the physical, emotional or financial help of my father.

My mother could see the challenges ahead and the role she played in navigating to her destination. She was determined that we would neither see nor live poverty. She was determined that we would make choices as girls and young women that would enable our lives to be easier than her own. She committed herself to creating a legacy that her children could be proud to represent. Through the grace of God and a wonderfully supportive extended family, my mother was able to create a good life for us in spite of my father's absence. She rewrote the script.

As hard as my mother worked to be both mother and father, she could not replace him. It is the law of nature. Women and mothers provide a set of tools and principles that are different from those of men and fathers. You just cannot be a daddy's little girl without a daddy! Mommy cannot do that for a little girl. When I became the parent of two wonderful boys, I realized that all those little events that I tucked away were weighing heavily on my soul. I realized that all of those events influenced the person I am today; the mother I am today; the friend that I am today and generally the way in which I see the world of male and female relationships. I knew that if I did not get past the resentment that I felt for my father, I would never release myself from the burden of pain. I needed to find the courage to understand him, to accept him, and to forgive him. I knew that I would be the ultimate benefactor of this sacrifice.

The youngest of eleven children, my father was loved and fiercely protected by his siblings and other family members. I have tried to write this book in a way that portrays him as I experienced and perceived him. This story is my truth. The truth is sometimes hurtful, especially if it is not the way we want to perceive and remember others, but the truth is what it is, the truth. I grew up fatherless when in fact I had a father who lived no more than fifteen minutes away. I had a father who chose not to participate in my life. That is the truth however unpleasant it may sound to some. Given that this truth is the truth, this story is about my truth. It is not about my father. I have, however, changed the names of many to provide and protect their privacy.

Finally, courage was necessary to lay myself open to the world in such a public manner as writing this book. For many years, I was ashamed to talk about my father and my journey through childhood without him. I was ashamed to say that I had a father, but didn't know him because he abandoned me. I believed that somehow others would judge me to be somewhat less than whole or broken because I grew up as an African American female from a broken home. Don't you love the phrase, "broken home"? What does it mean? I was always annoyed with statements like "children from broken home *this...*" "Children from broken home *that...*" I was not a broken child!

I am not an expert on the lives of women raised fatherless, but I am an authority, an expert and an "insider" to my experience, my feelings and my struggle to understand my legacy of fatherlessness and its impact on my life. I love my children so much that I cannot imagine not being a part of their lives by my own choice or otherwise. As you read this book, I invite you to consider the life choices you have made and those that you will make.

I want this book to cause women to consider the template that they have or will use to select the father of their children. I want women to consider their past, present and future as they define the life that their daughters will have with or without their fathers. As women, we make the choice. We decide. We select the men with whom we want to be involved. We may not always be the first to make the landing approach, but we decide who lands and who does not. Poor choices at the onset of a physical and emotional relationship will result in 'sperm donors' fathering our daughters.

It is critical that women, and especially black women, demand that their husbands or significant others play an active role in their daughters lives should their relationship produce children. We can give our daughters the information they need to desire those mates who possess the characteristics that will make certain that they formulate reasonable and educated choices. As mothers, we can lay a foundation for our daughters that will enable them to make thoughtful decisions.

I want this book to cause young women to disassociate themselves from behaviors that will result in unplanned pregnancy. I want young black women in particular to know that they have options for self-fulfillment beyond the charming prose of those whose attention focus on short-term physical gratification. As black women deserve and are entitled to be involved in loving and committed relationships.

I want young men to stop and think about the consequences of their actions as they participate in unprotected sex and other activities that create fatherhood if they are not ready to practice being a father. Stop the sperm donor approach to fatherhood. I want young men to understand that 'responsibility' means getting physically and emotionally involved in the development of the children they produce. I want young men to understand that fatherlessness and fragmented families are direct contributors to poverty in our communities. Children who grow up without their fathers are themselves more likely to repeat the cycle of fatherlessness, creating a revolving door of abandonment, hardship and poverty. I want men of all ages to understand that they play a vital role in their daughter's development and transition to adulthood.

Bill Cosby, in a recent commencement speech at Spelman College, encouraged young African American women to take charge and lead because African American males are not making the grade. Cosby told the graduates that the same male students who are dropping out of high school "have memorized the lyrics of very difficult rap songs." He added, "..and they know how to send their sperm cells out and then walk away from the responsibility of something called fatherhood." Mr. Cosby hits the nail on the head. Unfortunately, many of these young men did not have fathers from which to model their behaviors.

There was a compelling court case related to child support that drew national media attention. What made this case so compelling was the challenge it posed to the legal system that says fathers have a legal responsibility to provide financial support for their children. The case involved a young man who maintained he was not responsible for the financial support of his child because, following his girlfriend's claim that she could not be pregnant, they had had intercourse without contraception. To avoid the responsibility of providing support for the child, he had urged his girlfriend to abort the child but she refused and went on to deliver the baby. Therefore, when she sought child support, he filed a lawsuit. While the circumstances surrounding this case are unclear, the unfortunate by-product of two adults who behaved irresponsibly is a child who deserves to have both a mother and a father in his/her life. This father has indicated that he does not wish to participate in the child's life and is asking the court to release him of his legal responsibility. Irresponsible behavior created this scenario.

In an article published in The Michigan Citizen, Robert

Johnson, the head of the Georgia Fatherhood Services Network, speaks to another compelling issue around fathers and child support. His organization has prevented over 30,000 African American men from being imprisoned since its inception in 1997, for nonpayment of child support. "What we have in Georgia today is a fatherhood program in every town," he said, while attending an international fatherhood conference at the North-west Activities Center in Detroit, Michigan. His organization helps non-custodial parents find jobs and meet child support obligations by providing them with skills training in vocational schools. After going through the training, the state of Georgia places the train-ees in jobs in which they work while paying child support.

Dr. Jeffery M. Johnson, whose Washington DC based National Partnership for Community Leadership organization hosted the Detroit conference, calls it the condition of "the dead beat fathers," those who refuse to pay and "the broke beat fathers," those who can't find a job. The issue moves beyond the basic tenants of fatherhood to possible incarceration when the state must provide financial support through the child welfare agency and is unable to pursue payment from the father.

Another organization providing significant leadership and advocacy is the Fatherhood Initiative, Inc. in Gaithersburg, Mary-land. The organization does an outstanding job of bringing resources to individual fathers and support organizations whose mission is to foster families.

If this book does nothing else, I hope to persuade men, particularly young black men, to recognize what a critical role they play in the development of their daughters' lives. Put very simply, **daughters need their fathers**. Without their fathers, they have an incomplete life puzzle.

If you would like to share your story, please feel free to send an email to robin@robinwrightking.com or visit my website at www.robinwrightking.com.

You Were My Father, but Never My Dad

Half of my parentage belongs to you
Whether good, indifferent, or bad;
I always knew that you were my father
But I just wanted you to be my dad.

As a little girl many of my hopes and dreams
Were often tied up in hoping you'd come
To take me on that ever promised outing;
Let me get to know the man I'd come from.

As a teen I tried hard not to let disappointment show;
Put on a front like it didn't matter much,
But inside I wished that you'd find time for me,
That at least we could start to stay in touch.

I went to my prom then graduated with honors,
But your face I still could not see,
Many times I sat and pondered in tears
"Is what's wrong with our relationship me?"

To college I went and I felt so very proud
Of the greatest milestone I'd attained;
Maybe this would be the time that you would show up
But your absence was a fact that remained.

As I prepared to walk down the aisle to be wed,
I thought for sure that moment you'd share,
But I again had to face the undeniable fact
That my father was not going to be there.

My children were born; I had two wonderful sons,
Would a new generation change your mind?
Would you learn to be grandpa while you learned to
be dad?
Were you willing these treasures to find?

I finally came to terms as I looked down on your face
As you lay there handsome, even in death;
I made peace with my father though you were never
my daddy,
Knowing it's because of you that I draw every breath.

© 2006 Cassie P. Amos

www.blackpearlpublishing.com

Special thanks to my dear friend Cassie Amos, a wonderful poet, who without hesitation created the forward poem that so effectively, captures my emotions about my father. Cassie is the author of two books of poetry; *Verses for the Heart* and *Love, Life, and Surviving Loss*.

Debra, Charles & Robin, 1969

Chapter One – I Promise

"Not getting what you want is sometimes a wonderful stroke of luck."
— Unknown

I stopped dead in my tracks when I saw him. Butterflies instantly inhabited my stomach, frolicking about as if in a field of daisies. "Daddy! I think that's Daddy!" I thought without speaking.

As my sister Debra and I leisurely walked to the store on Tireman Avenue on this warm and sunny Detroit day to spend the twenty-five cents my grandmother had given to us, I saw two men standing in front of the neighborhood 'entertainment spot', the Blue Bird Inn. Even through the eyes of a child, the Blue Bird was a very populous place. It was common to see people gathered outside, hanging around in front whether night or day. Now, if you were wondering how a child of seven would know what went on outside of the Blue Bird after the streetlights came on, I will enlighten you. I did not *really* know! If you grew up as I did in a large urban environment, the streetlights were your signal to do something – run home! We knew that wherever we were at that moment, if the place was not home, we had better start making it in that direction. If we were bold enough to 'take our time' and my grandmother or mother had to call out for us, we knew that a sore behind was somewhere in our near future.

The Blue Bird and the activities inside and outside intrigued me. I guess I was attracted to it because of a need to understand what went on there. I can recall riding by in my mother's car, and peering out of the back window, trying to get a glimpse inside. The music always played loudly and the people were drinking, talking, and laughing. However, the inside always looked dark and mysterious; a contradiction I did not understand. The people were very different from the adults that I knew. The men wore flashy clothes with wavy processed or "conked" hair and the women wore tight clothes with shinny hairdos. They were always dressed as if it was a holiday, even on a weekday afternoon in July. Maybe, they had something to celebrate all the time. Whenever I had the opportunity to walk by, I would walk as close to the open front door as possible to get a look inside. I did so with fear and trepidation because I knew somehow that it was off limits to me. Who knew what really went on in there!

My sister, several steps ahead and realizing she was now walking alone, slowed and turned to look at me with a puckered brow and a question mark in each eye. Before she could scold me for not keeping up, I spoke.

"Debra, I think that's Daddy!" as I pointed to one of the two men in the distance, my eyes dancing and my heart pounding with excitement. Those butterflies in my stomach were in hot pursuit of something! She turned to look in the distance and spotted him as well.

"It is him!" she squealed with a similar level of excitement.

Our unique personalities were now in clear focus. My sister was not one to stand around and examine the situation like me. I was the thinker and she was the doer. At eight years of age and just 355 days older, she had clearly distinguished herself as the leader amongst our friends and most definitely of me. When we played games, she often expected to play the games she wanted to play and made clear those activities in which she did not wish to participate. When we watched television, she expected to watch the programs she wanted to watch. When we got new crayons, she expected to trade the *ugly* colors from her box for the bright pretty ones in my box! I was constantly on the defense trying hard to hold on to my position and my crayons. It was not easy and was often a losing battle. She was quick to state her position, take her position and to move forward. She always seemed to get 'there' first wherever and whatever first happened to be.

Without warning, she moved into action and took off running like a bat out of hell. I, on the other hand, labeled "*Miss Priss*" by my mother, usually took my time to analyze a situation, draw a few conclusions, and then act very carefully and gracefully.

Grace was particularly important because I never wanted to mess up my hair or clothes. On this day, we were true to form. Debra could not get 'there' fast enough. She would surely be first again. Allowing the wind to carry her, she left me a half a block away. Not wanting to be left behind, and excited to see my father, I trotted down the block, reaching the threesome to see my father bend down and hug my sister.

"Hey!" he bellowed in his deep voice, as he hugged my sister. Releasing her, he turned to give me an equally precious hug. "How are my pretty girls?" he said as he smiled so handsomely.

"Fine!" we shrieked in concert, jumping and shuffling our feet with excitement. What were those butterflies looking for? I thought as I stood staring up at him. He made me feel so special. My sister and I were grinning as if someone was taking our picture! I stood looking up at him very shyly, twisting, and wringing my hands because I did not know what to say or do. All I knew at that moment was that it felt so good to be standing next to him. He called us "*my pretty girls*". We belonged to him. Nothing else mattered. Time stood still. I was with MY DADDY!

"Where are you two going?" he said as he looked around to see if we were with someone. We did not notice the man he had been talking with move off to the side and enter the Blue Bird. We were in a world of our own, just the three of us.

"We're going to the store to buy candy! Gammy gave us a quarter!" my sister said eagerly as she reached into her pocket to show my father her quarter.

I smiled and followed suit, reaching into my pocket and displaying my quarter. To our surprise, he reached into his pocket, sorted through some coins, and handed each of us a bright shinny quarter. As he dropped the quarter into my hand, its motion slowed to liken molasses pouring. I watched it turn and glisten, catching the sunlight, as it descended to my hand. I smiled from ear to ear!

"Get more candy", he said as he looked into my eyes and smiled, reaching down to touch my chin. In that moment, I felt he saw inside of me. He seemed to understand my shy nature and my need for his attention. "You know you look just like my mother", he said with a warm broad smile. As I gazed back at him, I recorded his words and his touch in my mind forever.

The caution that I felt a few minutes before had dissipated and the butterflies had finally fallen asleep. I folded my fingers around the quarter and held it like it was a piece of gold. I was so grateful in that moment just to be with him, just to talk to him, and just to have him pay attention to me. I didn't know whether it was winter, spring, summer or fall. I had forgotten that we were standing in front of the Blue Bird and was completely unaware of the activity around me. My trance was suddenly broken when he spoke again.

"Debbie, you're looking more like your mother everyday", he said smiling at my sister as he pinched her chin. She grinned from ear to ear. Although we both looked like my father, my sister did bear a greater resemblance to my mother.

So there we were standing in front of the Blue Bird Inn show-ing our entire dental structure! As I looked at his face and into his eyes, I could see myself. I looked so much like him and I was so proud of that. I remember nervously surveying this tall slender man with caramel skin and beautiful straight black hair and thinking how handsome he looked. All of my senses were alive. I listened to his smooth voice and watched his broad smile as he continued to talk with us. I was in awe of him. I loved him.

"You girls know I love you", he stated. "I've been so busy working hard that I haven't had the time to come and see you but you know Daddy loves you, don't you?" he said again, very convincingly. These words I will remember for as long as I live. I didn't know then that words not married to their actions were meaningless.

Still beaming and nodding our heads to indicate 'Yes', we smiled. We did not know why he was not often with us nor did we really care in that moment. We wanted the moment to last for-ever. We were innocent to the knowledge that we had not seen him for several months because we had no real concept of time. We were oblivious to the fact that he had missed our birthdays and had not called or given my mother any assistance at Christ-mas. We were divinely unaware.

Squatting down to bring himself to our line of sight, he took each of us by one hand and said, "Why don't I come and get you girls on Saturday and we can go for a ride! Would you like that?"

We clung to every word! His words were like magic to our ears. A gift of forty-nine Barbie dolls and thirty-five Chatty Cathy dolls could not have outdone this proposition!

"Ooh! Yes!" we both jumped and shouted as we again shuffled our feet and bounced with excitement.

"Tell your mother I'll be by Sat—". Abruptly cut off by a call from across the street, my father turned to listen.

"Hey man! Where you beeeeeen? Ah been lookin' all over for you", the stranger shouted.

We turned to see a tall dark man walking slowly in parallel to our position on the opposite side of the street. In those few seconds that followed, I sized him up. I thought he was rude and I did not like the way he looked. He was dressed like the Blue Bird people, somewhat fancy and very shiny with wavy hair. He had a cigarette dangling from his mouth as he strutted in our direction, limping as if his leg was injured. We would later understand this to be the 'pimp' walk! If you were cool, you walked the 'pimp' walk.

My father turned quickly, flashing an enormous smile and began waving at the man. He slowly moved across the sidewalk toward the curb as he yelled "Hey man, wait for me! I'll be right there." He moved backwards to rejoin us but continued to communicate with his friend using hand signals to instruct him to wait. He knelt down in front of us, touched us both on our arms, and hurriedly said "You be good girls for your mother and Daddy will see you on Saturday. **I promise**." With that, he was gone.

We stood frozen and mute as he sprinted in slow motion across Tireman Street to join 'Mr. Rude'. I was crushed. Our journey along the yellow brick road had taken a sudden left turn. Someone had clicked my heels before it was time. I was not ready to return to Kansas! Suddenly, we were back in Detroit standing in front of the Blue Bird Inn. We watched my father and his friend laugh and talk as they walked in the opposite direction. We stood for a few moments in disbelief that he had appeared and disappeared so quickly. Realizing that our moment was over, we somehow sent a message to our feet instructing them to commence movement. In silence, we continued down the street to the candy store. We paused to look back several times, catching a glimpse of his diminishing stature as he moved further and further away. He never looked back. We watched until his distant figure became too small for our little eyes to see. He was gone.

The idea of buying candy was now not so exciting. I did not want to spend the quarter he had just given me because it was something from him that I could keep. It was symbolic of our brief yet celestial encounter. I slid the quarter into my pocket and made sure it rested securely positioned along with my other change and my championship set of jacks. We walked slowing toward our destination with the wind aloof from our sails. Arriving at the store, we looked around, investigating all of the wonderful sweet tooth opportunities. We spent only the quarter given to us by our grandmother and saved the quarter from our father. We bought red and green wine candies, squirrels, jawbreakers, and strawberry and grape Kool-Aid straws, each for a penny. The clerk placed our candy in little brown bags and we were off. I again slipped my hand into my pocket to find my quarter safely nestled with the rest of my items.   I did not want to lose my special quarter.

As we strolled back from the store eating our candy, we began to recuperate from my father's sudden appearance and disappearance. I could not help but look around the surrounding area for him as we passed the Blue Bird to return home. Maybe, he stopped along the way and we would have an opportunity to see him again. We were not so lucky. He had vanished.

As we got closer to home, disappointment began to give way to anticipation of the following day, Saturday. I suddenly realized that I wanted to get home as fast as possible to tell Gammy, my grandmother. Gammy was the name that we had given to her because we were unable as very young children to pronounce 'Granny'. I knew that she would be excited too! Unfortunately, I would have to wait a little longer to tell Mommy because she was working and would not be home for several hours. "I'll wear my favorite pink short set and my white sandals and ask Gammy to twist my hair instead of braiding it since this was definitely a special occasion", I thought. "Better yet, maybe she will put Shirley Temple curls in our hair!" Miss Priss was coming alive! I had my outfit and hair planned before we stepped one foot in the house. "I would look pretty for my Daddy tomorrow", I thought.

My mother and my sister and I lived with my maternal grand-mother from as early as I remember because my mother and father separated when I was less than a year old. In fact, I do not ever remember living in the same household with my father. My earliest childhood memories start at my grandmother's house where I experienced a wonderful childhood. We loved living with my grandmother because it was the focal point for the extended family. I can recall all of the wonderful holidays, especially Christmas Day when my aunts, uncles, cousins, and family friends would gather for dinner. Everyone bought presents and food and we enjoyed the laughter and music well into the late evening.

One of the favorite rituals was to have the children sing and perform for the adults after dinner. We would put on a record by the Supremes or the Temptations, sing along, and do the dance steps. I would usually decline to participate and if forced to do so, I would find a nice spot in the back of my cousins and make eye contact with no one! To say that I was shy was an understatement. My sister and my cousins were good, and they did not mind stepping out front, singing, and dancing their hearts out. I wanted no part of it because I was too skinny and could not dance as well as the others. As soon as the first song was over, I made a beeline for the bathroom and stayed there until they were done!

Even though I was too shy to do the singing and dancing routine, I enjoyed being with my cousins. My grandmother had thirteen grandchildren, nine of which were girls. We would play with our Barbie dolls and exchange their clothing, color in our coloring books, and play with our paper dolls. We would take turns spending the night at each other's homes and always looked forward to the next family event. We built, through our parents' example, a strong family spirit, and a loving foundation that has held our family together to this day.

My grandmother was a very strong woman who in a very quiet

and demure demeanor commanded respect and admiration. I remember her kindness and compassion. As my kids would say, I remember her 'straight up' spoiling us. We could get anything we wanted from Gammy because she was so sweet and so giving. We never took advantage of her but we knew how to get our way.

I always felt so connected to her because I believe she gave me what I needed most – attention. She was there to cuddle with me, to let me fall asleep on her lap, to let me play with her hair, and to put her arm around me and hold me as we watched the soap operas and game shows together. I was definitely a 'touchy feely' child. I enjoyed watching the *Match Game* with Gene Rayburn and *Concentration* with Hugh Downs, her two favorite programs. We would position ourselves in front of the television set; she in her green easy chair and cotton duster with me at her feet, at 4:00 p.m. each day to watch her programs.

I think my grandmother enjoyed giving me the attention I needed as much as I needed to receive it. I can imagine that she felt lonely after losing my grandfather and welcomed our presence in her life (as long as we were not too rambunctious!). I think that although we lived with her out of my mother's necessity, my grandmother enjoyed the activity in the house even though it created more work for her. My mother, with absolutely no support from my father, financial or otherwise, was able to provide a standard of living for us that was beyond that of most of our friends because we lived with my grandmother and she held a well paying job in the factory at Ford Motor Company. It was an arrangement that paid dividends of both parties. My mother was able to cover all of the household expenses (given the mortgage had been burned) and in turn my grandmother helped to care for us while my mother worked.

As we proceeded home, our minds were filled with Saturday and how much fun we were going to have.

"I wonder where he will take us," my sister said. "Maybe he will take us to Belle Isle and we'll get a chance to see the Big Stove. "

We loved to see the big stove because it was so large and so realistic looking that it was unbelievable. It was black with the fancy legs and as tall as a ten-story building. It almost made you believe in giants!

"I am sure that Belle Isle was where we were going. That's where we usually go for a ride when we go with Mommy", my sister said.

She was right, I thought. Whenever an adult talked about going for a ride, it was usually to Belle Isle or to the airport to see the planes take off and land. Yes. To see the planes take off and land! In the early 1960s, air planes were still a novelty in the Black community because very few people could afford to buy a ticket. We would park at the end of the runway and lay face up on the hood or trunk of the car to get the full experience. It was exciting!

Belle Isle, for a kid was also an especially exciting place to visit. It is located on the Detroit River between Detroit and Windsor, Ontario Canada, and is a beautiful island park with picnic grounds, a beach, a zoo, a planetarium, a lighthouse, horses, and other animals.

"You're right, we'll probably go to Belle Isle," I said with a big smile as I imagined all of the fun activities on the island.

We giggled and decided to run the rest of the way home, taking the short cut along the side of the Barber Shop and through the alley at Beechwood. As we neared our house, we raced up the alley past Mr. Williams' house, the Gardner's house and behind Mrs. Lawrence's house. We ran through our gate, past the garbage cans to the back door and into the kitchen breathlessly calling my grandmother, and slamming the back door loudly.

"Gammy, Gammy! Guess who we saw? Guess who we saw?" my sister shouted. Gammy was sitting in her favorite chair watching afternoon television, a.k.a. the soap operas. Unbeknownst to us, my little brother Marcus, who was only a year old, was sleeping.

"Shhh! Be quiet, your brother is asleep! He's only been down for a short time and I don't want him up yet!" my grandmother warned sternly, pointing her finger at us. We quieted down immediately because we did not want him to get up yet either.

Marc, short for Marcus, was all boy! He was rambunctious and wanted to be a part of everything we did. When we played with our Barbie dolls, he would plop himself down right in the middle of our elaborate set up that included a Barbie House, Ken and his sports car, Barbie custom made clothes and tiny little shoes. Of course, the Barbie shoes were a big attraction for him because they were so small and colorful. We were constantly pushing him away to avoid his fractious behavior that would ultimately result in the total destruction of our play area and a few missing shoes! Asleep was where we wanted him now so that we could have my grandmother's full attention. We were exploding with excitement.

"Gammy, we saw Daddy around the corner!" my sister whispered loudly as we sat down on the floor next to her green easy chair.

"He gave us a quarter and said he was going to take us for a ride on Saturday!" I interrupted, as I strained to keep my voice low while digging deep into my pocket to retrieve and show my treasure. "I want to wear my pink shorts and top and my white sandals. Ok? Ok Gammy?" I said. She could not get a word in edgewise.

"Yeah! He said he was going to take us for a ride! It is going to be so much fun. He'll probably take us to Belle Isle!" Debra said, whispering and chattering a mile a minute. "I'm going to wear my blue shorts and white sandals and I want to wear my hair down too, Gammy! Ok? Can you curl my bangs?" she said.

Bangs were a big thing back then. At the start of the day, our bangs were nicely curled, rolled under twice, and neatly positioned. By mid-day, the bangs usually expanded a bit and began to take wings. By early evening, they were drawn up, out of control, and air borne.

"Gammy, can you give us Shirley Temple curls? Please, please?" I said.

She was promising nothing. She did what she did best. She smiled and placated us by saying,

"We'll see. Let us talk to your mother when she gets home and see what she says. Now go outside on the porch and play so we do not wake up Marc. Go, go, go", she whispered hurriedly as she shooed us away toward the front door and on to the porch.

My grandmother did not seem too excited by our sighting and the day we had planned with my father. I wondered why. We were giddy with excitement. We could hardly wait for my mother to return home.

We parked ourselves on the bright colored floral green and white glider swing that adorned the porch of the old immaculately kept wood frame house and waited for her 3:00 p.m. arrival. We watched and waited. We glided back and forth, swinging our legs, only half-committed to playing with our Barbie dolls.

Wondering what time it was, I got up, walked to the screen door, and peered in to see Gammy watching television. "Gammy", I whispered. "What time is it"? She probably thought, oh God! Now they are going to play the 'what time is it' game all afternoon.

"It's quarter to three", she said pleasantly. Go sit down and play. Your mother will be home soon".

"How soon?" I questioned.

"Go sit down honey before you wake up Marc. She will be home soon, I promise". With that, I decided that there was no use in pushing her. What could she do but wait too.

My mother always knew that when we got to the curb where she parked before she did, we usually had something exciting to tell her. When we stayed on the porch and did not run to meet her, she knew that my grandmother had something to tell her that we did not want told. It usually meant trouble. On this day, we would beat her to the curb with wings on our heels and a song in our hearts. About fifteen minutes later as Gammy had promised, we sighted her yellow and black mustang cruising round the corner.

Debra yelled, "She's here! She's here!" In a flash, as usual, she was well ahead of me, down the steps and out to the curb. She got 'there' first again. I do not remember running to my mother's car; all of a sudden, I was on the curb alongside my sister.

"Mommy! Mommy!" we yelled as she motioned for us to move away from the curb so she could park without running us over.

"Get back so your mother can park!" my grandmother called from the front porch, watching as we hovered. "Give her a chance to get out of the car".

We paid no attention to her! This was too important. This was worth the risk of getting in trouble or even run over! We nested right on the edge of the curb with our toes tightly hugging the cement curb through our tennis shoes. When the car stopped moving and the engine purred to a halt, we lunged our bodies half way into the passenger side window and began to tell our story, both of us talking at the same time.

"Slow down girls. I can't understand you if you're both talking at the same time", my mother said.

"I'll tell her!" my sister said as she nudged me with her elbow.

As usual, I yielded and allowed her to talk. I didn't really have a choice anyway because she had already begun to speak as my mother uttered her last word. My sister proceeded to tell her about our 'Daddy' sighting, the invitation to go for a ride and a dissertation on our plans for wardrobe and hair. Still in the driver's seat of the car, she sat and listened.

"We'll see", she said as she got out of the car.

We knew what "we'll see" meant. It certainly did not mean yes and we were not taking no for an answer. I could not help but notice that she also did not share in our excitement. She was very reserved in her behavior just as Gammy had been. Again, I wondered why. Did she not want us to see our father? Maybe, she just did not understand. I had to make it clearer.

"Mommy", I called out as we ran after her, "Can we go? Can we go pleaseeeeeeeee?" I said feeling a sense of panic and desperation. It was now my turn to make a pitch. She could see how much this meant to us but I knew that she could not say no because she could not explain why. I imagine that she saw two little skinny, vulnerable girls with big brown eyes who wanted only for her to say yes. I made sure my eyes were as big as possible as I widened them to stare up at her.

She paused, looking at both of us for what felt like forever as we held our breath and finally said, "Ok".

The world was suddenly a brighter place! We began to jump

up and down with excitement but could not follow my mother into the house because Marc was asleep. Our mission accomplished, we wanted to tell our best friend Maria. We told each other everything! She had to be the first to know. We raced off down the street and again, I was surpassed by my sister who got 'there' first.

It was Friday night and we were full of anticipation. We gave my mother no trouble getting into the bathtub and getting out. We cooperated fully and even went to bed early without complaint. Quietly from the bunk beds in our cozily decorated bedroom, we whispered and chattered on about my father and our plans for the following day until we drifted off to sleep. All that mattered was getting to tomorrow. We were asleep in no time at all.

Saturday morning finally arrived. This was the day! It was on. My mother had to work so my grandmother helped us to get ready. Our clothes were starched and pressed to stand at attention; our lace trimmed ankle socks and our white sandals were ready; our hair oiled with "Royal Crown" grease, twisted into ponytails and embellished with white crisp ribbons. Our bangs were curled neatly into a tight roll and stabilized by a bobby pin. Excited about the day, we forgot all about the Shirley Temple curls. I know my grandmother was glad that we did not bring that up. We, of course, had no clue as to the amount of work that was required to transform us into two little brown Shirley Temples.

By 10:00 am, we had eaten our breakfast, made our beds, cleaned our room, helped my grandmother with the dusting, and dressed for the big day. We were particularly obedient and very cooperative that morning. We wanted nothing to stand in the way of seeing our Daddy. We perched ourselves on the bottom step of the front porch and quietly waited. Sitting on the bottom step provided a better view of the cars as they rounded the corner of our one-way street, Woodrow Avenue.

It was very quiet on the block as most of our friends were still toiling at their Saturday morning chores. Looking back, I realize now how spoiled we were. We had very few chores to perform. Our Gammy did everything for us. We were usually the last kids on the block to make it outside because my mother and grand-mother allowed us to sleep in on Saturday mornings and to watch cartoons until 11:00 am. We did not realize it at the time, but it was probably easier that we remain asleep or otherwise occupied and out of the way because of the family moving business run from my grandmother's home.

My grandfather and grandmother started one of the first African American furniture moving businesses in the city of Detroit, the G. W. Lloyd and Son's Moving Company, in the early 1920's. The business provided residential and commercial moving services throughout the Detroit metropolitan area and eventually across the United States. When my grandfather passed away in 1962, my uncle assumed control of the business, working alongside my grandmother. The business, run in part from the basement, required the movers to gather there for work with my grandmother busily assisting my uncle to dispatch the crew and the trucks to their various locations for the day. It was a crazy scene; one in which three young children surely did not belong. Therefore, we slept late and watched cartoons until the activity of the morning died down.

As we sat on the steps, fully engaged in our vigil, the silence around us was penetrated by the slam of a screen door in the distance. Mrs. Matthews had emerged from her house three doors down to water the beautiful flower garden across the front of her house. She had the best floral display on the block and a perfectly manicured lawn. She and her husband spent hours maintaining the flowers and caring for the lawn. Many of the children on the block thought she was a mean old woman because she would yell and threaten a spray from the garden hose if the children merely walked on her lawn or got too close to her flowers. It was unfortunately a circular situation where some of the more mischievous children on the block would taunt her as often as they could. They would purposely walk on her beautiful lawn right in front of her or even worse, they would ride their bikes across the lawn when she was not looking. The lawn was so perfectly sculpted that you could see the bike tire prints as they carved a mosaic design from one end to the other. The more she yelled at the kids, the more interested they became in annoying her.

The children eventually thought it would be more fun to pick her flowers rather than to bother with the lawn. The grass would always resume its natural position and stand at attention in no time, however her 'blooming wonders' were a different story! She treasured her flowers and took pride in their beauty year after year. Several of the neighborhood children began to make it a regular activity to pick the flowers after she went indoors for the evening. You know elderly people go to bed early so it was not difficult for the children to get to the flowers without being seen. The following morning, you could hear her yelling when she discovered her damaged flowers. It was so entertaining then to see her yell and scream at the 'suspects' as they passed by and politely spoke to her as if they were completely innocent. She always seemed to know the guilty parties. Of course, the kids would vehemently deny any involvement when their parents were informed.

As a child, all I saw was the comical aspect of Mrs. Matthews 'performance' for the block. You could hear her yelling half the way down the block. As an adult, I can now see how infuriating and disheartening it had to be to see her precious creations destroyed.

"Hi Mrs. Matthews", I called down the street.

"Hiiiiiiii" she called back as she waved to us, with the southern drawl that all of the older people seemed to have. We watched in silence as she tended to her flowers and tried to repair the damage. "These bad kids have picked my flowers again!" she yelled. The curtain was on its way up and the performance would begin!

My dad had not called to confirm the time he would pick us up; a little detail not shared with us. Not sure where my father was living, my mother left messages at several places asking him to call her to discuss his plans with us. He returned the call that evening telling my mother that he would phone my grandmother in the morning to give her a specific time. He did not make the morning call. After sitting outside for what seemed like an hour, I began to question silently what time he would arrive. Did we have the right day? Doubt was knocking at the door. "He said he was coming to take us for a ride on Saturday and Saturday is today", I thought. "I know he'll be here", I concluded, ushering the doubt away.

Beginning to feel impatient and a little bored, I decided that we needed to partake of one of our favorite past times – coloring.

"I'll go and get our coloring books!" I said to Debra as I got up to go into the house. "I'll ask Gammy if she knows what time Daddy's coming too".

As I opened the front door, I saw that Gammy was on the business phone so I ran up the steep staircase like lighting to our playroom to get the coloring books and crayons first. I knew exactly where to find them because in our house, everything had its place, even in the playroom, which really was not a separate room, but a play 'area', that was a very wide second floor hallway that ran along an outside wall and served as the entrée to two bedrooms. We spent a lot of time there particularly during the winter months playing with our toys.

I found the coloring books right away and the big 64 pack of Crayola crayons stacked neatly on the corner table in our play-room. With my items in tow, I raced back down the staircase, skipping every other step and dashed back to the front of the house where Gammy was still on the phone giving someone rates for moving.

"The cost for three men and a truck is...", I heard her say as I approached.

I stood in front of her very patiently, clutching my coloring books and crayons as she continued to talk. She turned to look at me for a moment but did not stop to address me. I knew what that meant. It meant 'get out of here and don't interrupt my call'.

"Do you have a piano?" she continued as the house line, the second phone line in the house began to ring.

She did not have to tell me to answer it. I was on that phone like it was my lifeline. "This could be Daddy", I thought.

"Hello!" I blurted loudly as I spoke into the big black receiver of the rotary dial phone.

Gammy was good at non-verbal methods of communication. She had that special body language and look that included the glare in the eyes, the stern upright posture, the menacing facial expression, the hands on the hips, etc., down to a science. She gave me one of those looks that simply said – 'I know you see me on the phone'. Making noise when she was on the business phone was not acceptable.

"Hi Robin, this is your Aunt Pat. How are you?" the voice on the other end said. It was my Aunt Pat, my mother's younger sister and the baby of the family.

"Hi Aunt Pat. I'm fine", I said in a now hushed voice while looking at my grandmother for her approval of my lowered voice.

"Is your mother home?"

"No she's at work today, but Gammy is here".

"She had to work on a Saturday?"

"Yep. She didn't want to go because she was tired, but she had to go because she said Ford Motor Company didn't care if she was tired,"

"Ok", she said as she chuckled. "Let me speak to Mother".

I turned and attempted to hand the phone to my grandmother. She was still on the business line so I don't know why I volunteered her presence without telling Aunt Pat that she was busy. She just stared at me and continued to talk.

"She's on the business phone right now. Are Donna and Rachel home?"

Not giving her an opportunity to respond to Gammy's unavailability, I wanted to tell my cousins Donna and Rachel about my father coming to pick us up.

"No they're not here. They've gone with their father today", she said.

"Oh! We're going with our daddy today too!" I said with excitement. "We're waiting for him to pick us up now. We're probably going to Belle Isle. He said he was coming to take us for a ride today when we saw him on our way to the store yesterday. I can't wait until he gets here!".

"Well I'm excited for you! I'm sure he'll be there soon", she said with assurance. "Tell Mother to call me when she gets a chance and I'll call you tomorrow and you can tell me all about your day with your father".

"Ok, bye".

I returned the phone to its cradle, smiling because I was

proud that I could talk about my daddy. Gammy was still on the phone so I could not talk to her to see if my father called and to tell her about Aunt Pat's call.

Before going back outside, I went to the kitchen to check the time because I had to have something to report when I went back to the porch with Debra. The clock on the big white stove said twelve o'clock! I could not believe my eyes. How did so much time pass? I thought. I felt panicked. Doubt was again knocking at the door. Did we have the right day? I ran back through the living room where Gammy was still on the phone. I paused briefly but realized there was no point in stopping to talk with her. I ran outside to the porch to tell Debra the news.

"Debra. Its twelve o'clock!" I blurted loudly as I burst on to the porch, causing the screen door to slam. My grandmother whirled around in her chair and gave me 'the evil eye' for the second time in five minutes. I decided to pipe down and sit down.

"It's twelve o'clock!" I blurted again in a low whisper. "He's not coming. I think he forgot about us!"

"He's coming. He said he was coming and he's coming", she said in an almost defiant tone. We sat silently for a few minutes, both wondering if he was really coming. We opened our Barbie coloring books and began to color in silence. The clock was ticking.

"Lunch time girls!" my grandmother called from the kitchen.

She was off the phone. We paused and looked at one an-other for a moment. I knew my sister was thinking the same thing I was thinking - that the moment we ventured off the step, he would come, and we would miss him because maybe he forgot where we lived or something would happen and we would not be there to see him. I could not remember my father ever visiting my grandmother's home so I was not sure he knew where we lived. My grandmother who appeared at the screen door to summon us again interrupted my thoughts.

"Girls, did you hear me? Your lunch is ready. I made your favorite egg salad sandwiches and butterscotch pudding".

She was right, it was our favorite, but we were not moved. We both slowly got up and entered the house as she held the door. She knew we did not want to leave our post. She knew how desperately we wanted to see our father and could not stand the thought of missing him.

"Can we eat out on the porch Gammy?" I said, knowing this was not allowed. Eating on the front of the house was "country" and uncouth, she used to say.

"We will miss Daddy when he comes", I said with a look that would break your heart. I am sure I did the 'big brown eyes' thing again.

She paused for a moment and said, "Your Daddy knows where you live. He has not forgotten. You girls go in the kitchen and eat and I will keep an eye out for you. I'll sit on the front porch. I won't move until you finish your lunch".

With that said, she did exactly what she proposed. She sat on the porch glider and talked with our elderly neighbor, Mrs. Lawrence, until we finished our lunch. We prayed that the business phone would not ring, drawing her away from 'our' post. We were covered for now.

My grandmother was such a wonderful woman. She was so special that I almost felt like she belonged to me. As a middle child, I often felt lost in the shuffle between my sister and brother. I did not reign as the first born with all the privileges it brings, nor was I the baby, still another special category with its own unique benefits. I was always the obedient 'good little girl' in the middle. I expected that good behavior would result in positive reinforcement and the level of attention that I needed. To my surprise, the concept worked in school, but did not necessarily work at home. In school, the 'effort equals reward' model worked very well. What a great deal! I worked at a moderate level, achieved good grades, and was rewarded with the appropriate level of attention; the honor roll, achievement certificates, stars on my papers, etc.

At home, the situation was a little different. The squeaky wheel usually got the oil and my brother was really squeaky! While not really misbehaving but behaving with the vigor and curiosity of any boy a year and half old, he was constantly the center of attention. If he wasn't in my mother's makeup using her lipstick to write on the walls, he was doing something really cute like dancing or trying to sing, but in either situation drawing attention to himself. He was the baby and everyone looked to him to share in his discoveries and to provide the guidance he needed. Now, Gammy was sixty-seven years old, so Marc's antics were usually met with little resistance as she cared for us during the day when my mother was working. He was a very cute little boy and very spoiled.

My sister, on the other hand, was not only the apple of my mother's eye, but she typically acted and reacted according to the rule of 'Debra' instead of the rules that everyone else followed. Consequently, she required direction and monitoring. In short, the girl was 'fass' and fast! She was never afraid to speak up and to speak out and was always heard!

Now I was no angel, but I was simply more manageable because I wanted so much to please others, to be liked, and to be accepted. I, however, projected such a strong persona of independence that those who needed to know that I needed the attention were often unaware. Somehow, my Gammy always knew. She was just automatically there, anticipating and providing the support and attention before I even knew that I needed it. She seemed to have a window into my soul that no one else had.

We ate our lunch very quickly and found our places again on the bottom step to continue our surveillance.

"That was pretty fast girls. Did you finish your lunch that quickly?"

"Yes. We ate really fast so that we could get back out here", my sister boasted.

I simply shook my head to indicate yes, because my mouth was gaping with food that I stuffed in to keep up with Debra. She, of course, finished before me.

"We were afraid that the business phone would ring and you would have to leave the porch to answer it", she added.

"I'm going back in to finish my paper work. I want you to stay right out front", she said. She waved to Mrs. Lawrence and went back into the house. Did she think we were going somewhere? Our bottoms were glued to those steps!

It was 12:45 PM when we left the kitchen after lunch. With the sound of each approaching car, we stood up to get a look hoping it was Daddy arriving so that we could begin our adventure.

"What kind of car does Daddy have?" I asked Debra, realizing that neither of us knew what he drove.

She turned quickly with a look as blank as a clean sheet of paper. It never dawned on us to know what kind of car we were looking for. We had no idea what kind of car my father had, but we figured that he must have one because he was coming to take us for a ride. Another car. Not him. Another car. Not him. Another. Not him. Not him. Not him and not him. Car after car passed, as did the time, but none even slowed to tease our heightened expectation.

As a screen door slammed in the distance, we heard a familiar voice.

"Hey y'all", she yelled as she ran down the street toward us. It was Maria. "What y'all do'in? How come you guys are just sitting here", she said as she looked at us curiously.

"This is the day that our Daddy is coming to take us for a ride. Do you remember what we told you yesterday? We're just going to sit here and color in our coloring books until he comes because we don't want to get our clothes dirty," I said.

"When is he coming? I hope he doesn't come too soon

because I won't have anybody to play with when you leave", she said with a sad face.

Debra and I looked at her and shrugged our shoulders to indicate that we did not know what time he was coming. Maria had no way of understanding how important this day was to us. She had a father who lived with her. She was the youngest of three children and the apple of her father's eye. We often watched when her father returned home from work each day; Maria would run to the car and give him a hug. He often had a surprise for her like a piece of candy or a new toy. They had a special relationship. She had as many toys as we did and lots of really nice clothes. She always seemed to have plenty of candy money and was always willing to share the candy she bought or anything else that she had. She was a good friend. If we had fifty cents, she had a dollar. She seemed to be able to do anything she wanted and got everything she asked for. We really looked up to her. "Well I guess I'll go and get my coloring book too", she said as she missiled off down the street toward home. She returned moments later with her coloring book and a 120 pack carton of Crayola crayons.

Another car. This one we recognized. "Oh my God", I thought as all three of us stood up to look.

"It can't be", I thought aloud.

We all stood in silence. The car slowed and proceeded to park in front of the house next door. I could not believe it. My sister and I stood rigid in disbelief. Maria sat back down, and looked up at us wondering why we continued to stand in silence with a sad look on our faces. My mother was home from work. Was it really 3:00pm already? She got home from work each day at 3:00pm. This could only mean one thing. More than half the day was gone already and he had not come.

"He's not coming," I said to Debra as I tried to hold back the tears.

As she turned to look at me, she was already crying silently. She knew as well. Debra was visibly more excited than I was through this entire process, so it would stand to reason that she would be more passionate in her disappointment. I was guarded and careful not to show too much disappointment, although inside I was devastated at the idea that he was not coming. As I watched my mother park, I kept playing the previous day's scene in my mind where he clearly said 'I will pick you up on Saturday'. It was simple; today is Saturday and he said he would take us for a ride on Saturday. At seven years old, this was logical. What could we have confused? I believed him; I trusted him; I needed to be with him; I needed my father to take us for a ride.

"Daddy's not coming", I said softly again choking back my tears.

Maria did not know what to say but she kept quiet because she could see how hurt we were even if she didn't understand.

We did not run to meet my mother at the curb as we had done the day before and as we did on most days when she returned from work. She looked surprised to see us sitting on the step. I could see her watching us as she parked the car, knowing that something was wrong. As she got out of the car and approached the porch, she knew what was wrong. We could see it in her eyes and she could see it in ours.

"Hi girls" she said with a cautious tone, getting close enough to see the tears. "What's wrong? Did your father come?" she asked looking first at my sister and then at me.

We both looked up at her with big teary eyes and shook our heads 'No'. Her caution and apprehensive tone immediately turned to anger.

"Damn-it!" she cursed and dashed up the stairs and into the house, calling my grandmother. "Mother!" "Mother!" "What happened?" "Where is Charles?"

Although I could not hear my grandmother's response because their voices were now muffled as they moved toward the back of the house and into my grandmother's bedroom, I could hear the emotion in my mother's voice. Debra and I tiptoed on to the wooden porch and pressed our faces to the screen to try to hear what they were saying. My mother was very upset. I could hear her crying. I'm sure my grandmother told her that we had been sitting on the porch since 10:00 am, refusing to budge, except to eat and to 'visit the facilities'. I then heard the sound of the rotary dial phone, as someone, probably my mother, impatiently dialed each number. After a few moments of silence, I heard the receiver slam into its cradle. We heard more of the muffled talking, more impatient dialing, the receiver slam, and silence again. The voices were now getting closer as they emerged.

"I called him last night and told him that he had better not disappoint these kids! He said that he would be here," my mother cried. "I can't believe that he would do this!"

With our faces glued to the screen, we did not try to run to hide the fact that we had listened to their conversation. We were frozen with the fear and realization that he might not come after all.

When I think back about that day, I cannot help but remember how hurt we felt. We, of course, didn't understand why it was such a painful experience other than we wanted what we wanted; we wanted our father to come and spend the day with us as he had promised. I know now that what we were experiencing was unconditional love for my father even though he did nothing to contribute to our lives and well-being. He was our father and 'father' means loving without limits. It means loving even though we never got a birthday card, never a phone call, nothing, but we still loved him. We didn't know what having a father was really about but we understood enough about the role at this stage in our lives that we belonged to him and he to us. Where was he?

As an adult with children of my own, I can only image my mother's pain. We were hurting and she could not fix it. She created, as most parents do, a predictable environment for us that she managed well. She worked hard to fill the gap left by my father's absence. On that day, in crept my father with empty promises and hurt. The predictable world that she had created had been penetrated. She was apprehensive about allowing this venture, but she knew that she could not say no. She knew what we did not know. She knew that he was unreliable. As a mother wanting very much for us to have a caring father in our lives and wanting us to see him because we wanted to see him, all she could do was to manage the fallout from his broken promises.

We sat on the porch; two pretty little girls with outfits still crisp and clean, white ribbons and white sandals, until 5:00 p.m. when Maria had to go home for dinner. We went in around the same time and ate dinner as well in silence. My mother and grand-mother tried to make conversation with us, promising to take us for a ride the following day. I smiled politely and nodded yes to my mother's invitation. Debra was having no part of it. She was too upset to consider an alternative. It was simply not the same. She did not respond.

'I hear footsteps on the porch', I thought. Without asking permission to leave the dinner table, I flung myself to the front door.

"It's him! I know it's him!" I shouted.

Before I could get to the door, the doorbell rang. Time stopped. 'It was him! He had not forgotten', I thought. 'He did come'. My mother immediately got up and paced vigorously behind me. The few moments that it took us to find our way to the front of the house seemed like forever. I was hyperventilating by the time I got to the door. It was not him.

"Hi Maria", my mother said before I could speak. "Debra and Robin will be out in few minutes when they finish their dinner".

"Ok. I'll wait on the porch" I heard Maria say as she plopped down on the glider.

I exhaled with disappointment and proceeded slowly back to

the dinner table, where I looked at Debra who already knew that it was not him. She barely even looked up. My mother stepped behind my sister's chair and kissed her on the cheek.

"I'm so sorry girls. I'll make it up to you. When I get a hold of him, he's going to get a piece of my mind. Let's all get ice cream when the ice cream man comes later this evening. Ok?" my mother said.

We both looked up long enough to nod 'Yes' and returned to our dinner. Under normal circumstances, this 'nodding' business would not fly. Anything other than a clear Yes or No was disrespectful and would result in a stern glare or even 'corrective action'.

We slowly crept through the eating process and returned to the outside to play with Maria. She helped us to recover from the disappointment without knowing it. She bought a sense of normalcy back to the day in that she got us back in the 'play' groove. In no time at all, for the first time that day, we moved off the steps and back into our normal world of play. The Mr. Softie truck came by and my mother brought ice cream for us as promised.

As the sun slowly began to close its sleepy eye, and darkness ebbed the sky, our attention focused upon the bright insect like eyes of each car that crawled our street.

Not him. Not him. Not him.

Chapter Two – Till Death Do Us Part

"Our lives are shaped as much by those who leave us as they are by those who stay." — from *Motherless Daughters: The Legacy of Loss,* Hope Edelman

When I got the phone call on October 4, 1995, that I needed to get to the hospital as soon as possible, I was stunned. Nestled into the comfortable surrounding of my office cubicle, I was immediately alarmed to hear my half sister Kenya's voice on the other end of the line. I could tell by the excited tone in her voice as she began to speak, that something was wrong. It had to be my father.

I had gotten a similar call from my half sister Trina just two weeks prior when she phoned to tell me that my Dad was hospitalized. I immediately dropped everything and met Trina and Kenya at St. John's Hospital. When we arrived, we each took turns visiting; I believe two at a time. I had not seen him for at least a year and was surprised by his appearance. He was very thin, frail, and looked nothing like the person I had seen a year ago. He was connected to an oxygen machine and breathed long and slowly as he glanced around the room. He looked like a man well beyond his 62 years. Apparently, years of smoking had taken its toll, enlarging his lungs and causing the symptoms of emphysema. The weight loss was obvious as was the labored breathing even when lying down.

I spoke to and embraced his wife and my half sister Karen. It was so refreshing to see Karen. She was like a bright ray of sunlight at the dawn of a summer morning with the whole day left to shine. I had not seen her in some time and was fascinated to see that she had grown into a beautiful young lady. I believe that she was a high school senior at the time and was anticipating graduation and acceptance to the University of Michigan. Seeing her made me think of myself at the tender age of seventeen with my whole life in front of me. As I observed her, I thought about the choices she would make in her life and how she would fare should something happen to my father, her father. I wondered about the relationship she had with my father; her father. Had he been a better father to her than he was with me? Had he been there when she learned to walk? Had he been there on the first day of kindergarten? Had he been there when she went on her first date? Was he there? I knew that my father left the marriage and their home for some period to pursue another relationship. How did she manage my father's absence at such a young age? Did she know of all of her half brothers and sisters? How much did she know about my sister and me? Did she know the truth about our lives and the role that her father; my father played or didn't play? Watching her, I felt an instinctive need to know her. I wanted to be a part of her life in some way; however, life's circumstances would dictate another avenue.

It was obvious that she had a mother who moved to fill the gap as my mother had done for me. She had a mother who provided the love and direction that she needed. She had a mother who had undoubtedly offset the loss with the natural and instinctive extension of love and caring that a mother could give, just as my mother had done. I silently wished her well, knowing that she would be a successful and productive young woman.

My father was clearly having difficulty breathing, speaking in a very hushed and husky voice.

As I approached the bed again, his wife moved to his bedside and said, "Charlie, Robin is here."

I reached for his hand and spoke to him. "Hi Dad", I said, leaning over him.

He recognized me and tried to speak, but was encumbered by the oxygen equipment that covered his nose and mouth.

He smiled and said in an almost inaudible whisper, "Robbie".

"Don't try to talk, you need your rest".

He looked up at me and smiled. He was too weak to talk. As I looked at him, smiling, I thought about the familiar way in which he addressed me, the familiar way in which he always addressed me by calling me 'Robbie'. I cannot remember him ever calling me anything but Robbie. Do not get me wrong; always does not suggest that he called my name or some derivative of my name often. It simply means that in the scattered and significantly infrequent times that I spent with my father, he always called me Robbie. This familiar address struck me because I don't believe that anyone else ever addressed me in this way. A name uniquely his, 'Robbie' had an especially endearing ring when spoken by my Dad, almost sounding as if he was addressing a small child or puppy. It surely sent the message I wanted to receive, regardless to how reckless his behaviors were as a father and regardless to the true basis under which the familiar name emanated; guilt. It was the guilt that an absent parent would experience if they had been nothing more than a sperm donor. You know how the story goes. Out of sight, out of mind, but in sight, the need arises to clear one's conscience by making excuses for truancy. Inadequacies that we choose to ignore don't bring us much pause. However, coming face to face with a child or children that are of your making and to whom you have not been a father, should give rise to anxiety and conduct piloted by guilt. The deficient parent's credo is to find ways to make one feel better for all the things they haven't done by overcompensating with whatever it is they have in which to make a payment. Calling me 'Robbie' and behaving in a very familiar manner was his method of payment. Unfortunately, any payments he made were one time emotional deposits or credits toward a negative balance that will never zero out let alone ever move to the positive column. As a child, I was willing to grab a hold of the slightest shred of evidence that he felt a paternal connection or any kind of connection. I was too young then to understand this payment thing, but as an adult, I was not quite so gullible.

I understood the guilt deal and was not necessarily willing to allow him to make a deposit. I was never ever rude to him, but because I felt hurt by his absence, I could not forgive him and it came through in my spoken and unspoken communications with him. I had trouble embracing him emotionally as my father. I felt distant, disconnected and annoyed when he over compensated. I simply could not help him with his guilt or his need to make a deposit, even in his illness. I could not forget.

On this day, I did not feel distant, disconnected or annoyed. It was interesting to think at that moment just how my name sounded coming from lips. His voice was so low that I had to lean into him, as he lay upright in his hospital bed. I wanted somehow for him to be able to say my name the way I had heard him say it before with his strong baritone voice and his broad smile as it slowly crept across his face. I did not know on this day that this would be the last time I would hear his voice. As hurt as I had been for most of my life by him, I did not want to see him like this. It was painful.

I had seen my father about a year before at my half sister Trina's home in Toledo for a Labor Day cookout. When Trina invited me, I wanted to ask her if he would be there but did not. I had a feeling that he would be. He had always been at Trina's home for previous gatherings so I guessed that he would be there. I was a little uncomfortable about seeing him on one hand, but looking forward to it on the other because I wanted my boys to see their grandfather. They had only seen him once or twice but because they were young, they did not remember him. When I think back about wanting the boys to see him, I question my purpose. What did I want them to see or experience. I surely didn't want them to see the person I saw, the absent father and now absent grandfather. Maybe, I wanted them to see the glossy version of a man who really didn't exist. I believe I wanted them to see him as their grandfather so that they could really know that he existed, if only for a brief moment. I wanted them to experience that innate quality that grandfathers have to welcome and embrace their young. I wanted them to experience with him what I didn't experience. I was again lost in that chasm of desire and fiction.

The cookout was well underway when we arrived. The driveway was full of cars, requiring that we park half a block away. As we approached the house, we could see the younger children running circles around the house and the older children playing basketball. I could see the excitement in the boys' eyes as they spotted the children and all of the activity. We could smell the aroma of barbecue on the grill and hear music playing. As the boys clung to my side, several family members who I had not seen in sometime greeted me. Making my way into the house, I heard his unmistakable voice. I was instantly nervous. Why? Was I looking for his acceptance and approval again? Was he going to be any different than he had been the last time I saw him? I was sure that today he would be successful in making a deposit not only with me but with the boys as well.

Moving closer to his voice and into the family room, I saw him.

I was aghast by his appearance. I didn't look well. I remembered that he didn't look well the last time I saw him, about a year before, but I attributed his appearance to his drinking. As I scanned his body, I saw something unfamiliar. I saw what looked like a portable oxygen tank. It took a minute to comprehend what 'it' was and to see that 'it' was connected to him. He was sitting on the family room sofa with his wife and Karen with the oxygen tank mask sitting in his lap. He looked up as I entered the room, immediately recognizing me.

"Robbie", he said with a weak smile and that 'I know I've done wrong' look on his face that I had seen so many times before.

He motioned with a wave for me to come over. As I leaned over to say hello and kiss him on the cheek, I noticed how thin and frail his body had become. He was so small and gaunt that he appeared sunken into the sofa. His face was exceptionally slender and the bags under his eyes were exaggerated and swollen. His hair seemed straighter than before probably because of the thinning and graying brought on by age. He was now 61 years of age. I would learn that he suffered from emphysema and his lungs had been badly damaged by the disease. His voice, though weakened, still echoed a pretty strong and commanding tone.

"Hey Robbie, how's my girl?" he said, holding the oxygen mask in his hand.

"I'm fine Dad. How are you?"

I felt pretty dumb asking that question because it was clear that he was not doing well, but my response created an opportunity for him to talk and for me to listen. His wife motioned to my half sister Karen to get up to allow me to sit down next to my Dad. I sat next to him as he began to speak.

"Well, I'm not doing so well. My emphysema is really acting up, so I need this oxygen in case I fall short of breath. I have to take it with me wherever I go. But I'm ok, except for the shortness of breath".

I didn't really know what to say. I felt embarrassed that I had not known of his illness and its severity before this day. It was such an unnatural feeling to be sitting so closely with him and at the same time to feel so uncomfortable and disconnected from him.

I could see the depth of the illness and the pain in his eyes as he drew each breath. I felt so sorry and afraid for him. As we continued to talk, the battle inside me began to rage. I wanted to reach out to him physically to express the feelings that I could not articulate. I did not understand my feelings enough to express them. It was not love, I told myself because I didn't love him. I did not know him. I didn't know this man that I had just called 'Dad' a few moments ago. Still I wanted to care about him and love him because he was my father. I should care about my father and love him, I kept telling myself, but life's circumstances had altered this natural relationship. I was frozen for those few moments trying to win the battle. 'I couldn't love him. I refused to love him, I thought. I had nothing from my past to draw upon to help me to stabilize my feelings or to pick sides in the battle. I had nothing to look to but the pain and memories of abandonment.

I thought about my mother who had lost her life to breast cancer four years earlier. I wondered why he had been spared and why she was taken away from me. I wondered why the other side of my natural connection felt so unnatural. I simply did not know this man.

Removing myself momentarily from the conversation, I drifted back to the voices and laughter surrounding me. I listened to the bits and pieces of conversation fragmented by the rambunctious movement of children running about the room and a sudden outburst of laughter as two cousins embraced greeting each another after a long absence. I smiled as I watched everyone enjoying themselves and was glad that we came. It felt like a family reunion. I decided to get up to get some food for the boys and myself and talk with my other relatives.

Returning, I realized I was winning the battle. I was detaching and not allowing my sympathy for his illness to change my feelings. I did not want to cave in and push aside all of the hurt I felt. I deserved to hold on to that pain and to hold it over his head ever so silently. I could not and didn't let it go. Feeling increasingly uncomfortable, I decided to switch gears.

"Dad, did you see the boys?" I said, changing the subject.

"Oh, the boys! Where are they?"

I motioned to Ricky and Ryan who had upon entering the room, moved to the sliding door that led out to the back yard where their cousins played. Ryan was drawn to the outdoors, but Ricky stood silently watching his grandfather and me as we spoke, almost in awe. With the boys responding to my call and moving in our direction, my father focused his attention on Ricky, twelve years old at the time, because he looked so much like a 'Wright' as I did.

"Hi young man", he said to Ricky, smiling. "You're really growing up! How's school?" he said.

After a few moments of their exchange, I realized that he never called Ricky by his name. He kept calling him 'young man' and not by his first name. Wow! He didn't know his grandson's name!!!! Even if he could not distinguish between them who was Ricky and who was Ryan, I would have expected that he knew their names. Sad. When I summoned the boys to come over, I had not called them by name. I decided to let him off the hook.

"Dad this is Ricky", I said as he shook Ricky's hand, "and this is Ryan".

"Hi Ricky, he said, completing his hand shake with Ricky. "Hi Ryan", he bellowed in his deep but weakened voice.

The boys nodded respectfully, shaking his hand as he reached for them. They both looked sort of 'star stuck' as if they had just met a movie star. My Dad was in awe of them as well because they had grown so much since he had seen them two to three years prior. We continued to talk about the boys as he asked their ages and grade in school. Feeling a little uncomfortable with a pregnant pause in the conversation, the boys excused themselves to play with their cousins.

I continued to chat with my father and he promised as usual

that he would call and come to visit the boys. I told him he was welcome anytime, as usual. I was glad the boys had moved away because I didn't want them to hear his promise to visit. We exchanged phone numbers and he of course never called or visited, as was expected. I never called or visited either, also as usual.

As my mother had done for me, I spoke very little of my father to my sons. When they asked why their grandfather did not come around, I simply told them that he had issues in his life that prevented him from having a relationship with me, but 'oh how lucky' they were to have such a wonder Dad. They, of course, wanted to know of the issues, but I always told them, as my mother told me, that I would explain as they got older and were better able to understand. Somehow, even through all the pain, I wanted to protect his image in their eyes hoping for them to have at least a neutral image of him. He didn't make that an easy task. Further creating confusion and question, was the fact that they also had their paternal grandfather and two-step grandfathers. Who were all of these people? Most of their friends had two grandfathers but they had four.

Their paternal grandfather, Robert Brown, deceased in 1997, was a very loving grandfather. While he didn't spend a great deal of time with them because of health problems, they knew him as 'grandfather' and he was recognizable in that role. He easily played the role of family patriarch, husband, and grandfather. As grandfather, he was always there whenever the boys visited, not really doing much to establish himself as an authority figure and a protectorate other than to just be there. He held them when they were babies, played with them as toddlers, and talked with them as young boys. In their eyes, he was a father to their father. They understood and respected that relationship. They bore witness to the advice he gave to his son. They listened as he questioned their father about the condition and repair of our automobile. They remember his insistence that we have a full tank of gas before starting our twenty-five minute trek home from his house. They felt special because his genuine love and affection for them came through in every encounter with them. He was their grandfather and they knew him as such.

Grandfather number three is my stepfather Kenneth. He married my mother when I was twelve years of age and played the most active role as their paternal-grandfather because we maintained a close relationship even though he and my mother divorced after eleven years of marriage before the boys were born. Living close to us, he was then and is still a very active part of our lives. Affectionately called 'Brother Moes' by the boys, he has been involved in every aspect of their lives. He was there for every birthday party, for most of their sporting events, their graduation ceremonies, and more. He has played an important role in their lives, giving them an opportunity to have a strong and positive male figure from their extended family.

Their fourth grandfather, Mel, married my mother when I was twenty-six; a year after Ricky was born. He spent a lot of time with the boys when they were younger because we spent a lot of time at my mother's house. A wonderful man, he enjoyed playing with the boys as much as they enjoyed playing and climbing all over him. He unfortunately became significantly less active in our lives after my mother's death in 1990. He has since moved to New Jersey to be closer to his family.

After leaving the cookout, the boys had many questions about my father. They again wanted to know why they never saw him. They wanted to know if I was mad at him or if he was mad at me. They wanted to know if they should call him 'Charles' or 'Grandfather'. I suggested they call him 'grandfather' although I knew that it really didn't make a difference. Were they going to see him again anytime soon? Probably not. They also didn't understand the oxygen equipment and why he appeared to be in such poor health.

Also quite puzzling to them was the relationship between my half-sisters and I. Who was Trina and how was she my half-sister? What was a 'half-sister' anyway? Why did we have different mothers? Who was Kenya and how was she their aunt? Why did she have a different mother from Trina and from me? Did my mother know the other mothers? Who were their cousins and why did they not see them more often? Why? Why? Why? It was almost overwhelming! Their questions were certainly valid and posed in such an honest and curious manner; in a way that only a child could. As much as I wanted my father's "mess" to miss my boys, it was not possible. I knew, as they grew older they would continue to ask the questions and draw their own conclusions as I had done.

Driving hurriedly to the hospital, Kenya's voice and words

reverberated in my mind. 'Get to the hospital now' she said. "Trina and I will meet you there!" I felt panicked and fearful that he had already passed away. I had been in this same position, four years before, receiving a call from my step father Mel at 6:00 am on a Saturday morning directing my sister Debra and I to the hospital immediately because my mother had taken a turn for the worse. My sister who lived in Minneapolis in 1981 was in town to visit my mother because she was so ill and getting worse by the day. When we arrived at the hospital, we discovered that my mother had already experienced her transition. In fact, she had passed away just prior to the initial phone call placed by my stepfather. She was gone. Was my father gone already? I did not bother to ask Kenya how she knew that something was wrong. I was petrified.

How could I feel this way about a man I did not know? A man I did not love. How could I feel this way about a man who did not care to know me, a man who clearly did not love me? What was I feeling? As I drove, I felt anger for having feelings at all. I was not supposed to feel anything. I had trained myself to stop feeling for him a long time ago. I wanted to be numb. I felt victimized again – how could he do this to me? How could he make me feel this way?

While waiting for the hospital valet to take my car, I wiped my tears, reapplied my lipstick, and straightened my hair that was wind-blown by my mad dash to the parking deck to get to my car. I cleared my mind of the anger and all the feelings I did not understand and moved rapidly to the lobby to find Kenya and

Trina.

We arrived within two minutes of one another and proceeded to the front desk where we were given passes and directed to the elevator. Upon locating his room, we were shocked at what we found. The bed was empty and freshly made. We stood staring at the empty bed in disbelief as if he was going to appear any moment. I am sure we all thought that he transferred to another room or that perhaps we had the wrong room number. I think we literally stood there for 30 seconds in complete silence and disbelief. Just then, a nurse walked in and we inquired as to his whereabouts. She looked as stunned as we did. We knew something was wrong. We could tell by her body language and her delayed response that she was to be the bearer of bad news. She reluctantly told us that he had passed away several hours earlier and was in the hospital morgue. She apologized and asked if she could do anything for us.

We stood in the hallway in disbelief with our feelings scattered about. Each of us began to cry silently as the nurse continued to comfort us. What had happened? When did it happen? Why didn't someone call us? While I did not expect to get a call related to his health, I would have expected that someone would have called Trina. I believe she was especially devastated because she was closest to him and had visited with him in the days prior to his death. Trina had always gone out of her way to have a relationship with my father. She had grown up down the street from my father's brother, and was always there for him. She should have gotten a call.

I then learned from Trina that our rush to the hospital began when Trina phoned the hospital that morning to see how my father was doing but did not get an answer in the room. Calling the nurses station, she was told she needed to speak to my father's wife who was not in the hospital room at the time. Trina immediately knew that something was wrong and contacted Kenya who in turn phoned me.

Once we composed ourselves, we went to the nurses' station and learned that his wife had instructed them to move his body to the morgue because all of his family members had attended his body. We were again astonished. We could not believe that he was gone but we were even more astounded to find out in this way.

We composed ourselves in the lobby and decided to go to his home to offer our condolences. Surely, the family would be gathered there. We went initially with disappointment and anger. As I drove alone in my car to his home, I began to question the validity of my thoughts and emotions. Was I being selfish? Why had I wanted to see him just prior to his death when I didn't make an effort to see him before? Why had I allowed my feelings of anger to dissipate on that day? I knew the answer.

When we arrived at his home, we talked briefly before ringing the doorbell, and decided to put our feelings aside concerning the way that we learned of his death because surely this was a highly emotional event for his wife and our half sister Karen. Any comment or question about our exclusion on that day would only cause a problem that no one needed at such a difficult time. His wife had a full plate in handling her own grief and managing the pain that I am sure existed for Karen. I thought of Karen and wondered how she was dealing with her father's death. Of all of his children, Karen probably suffered the most in that he lived in the same household with her until his hospitalization and death. At seventeen years of age, death is a very heavy burden to carry because you are just old enough to truly understand and appreciate its finality.

When we arrived, the mood was upbeat but initially a little distant. We spent a few hours visiting with family members who had gathered.

He was gone.

Chapter Three – To Be Worthy of Your Love, My Child

"When I was a child, I spake as a child, I understood as a child, I thought as a child, but when I became a man', I put away childish things"
— I Corinthians 13

A father is the first 'significant other' in the life of his daughter. He is the first man in her life honored with her love, trust and affection, and he is the first man she wants to love her in return. A father's role in the life of his daughter is uniquely exclusive. He has an exceptional opportunity to sculpt her vision of the world, to establish himself and his 'maleness' as the cornerstone for strength, guidance and protection, while creating a template for relationships with other men in her life. Fathers provide their daughters with the sustenance to define male-female relationships and to set expectations for the men that she will encounter in her adult life. He is a role model, whether he is a good father or not.

The most pivotal role fathers play in the lives of their daughters is the influence they have during adolescence. It is during this period that girls begin to process what healthy male-female relationships are about. Girls who have fathers who are involved in their lives are more likely to have age appropriate relationships with boys during this period. They develop a more wholesome approach to 'boyfriend-girlfriend' relationships with well-established boundaries as influenced by the father-daughter relationship. They have a greater sense of these relationships and their potential to move to the next level. They see the role their fathers play and consequently begin to develop a model for what is appropriate and acceptable to them and their parents based on their parents' expectations and accountability to their wishes.

As an absent father, both physically and emotionally, I idolized my father because I chose to see him as an icon symbolizing all of the wonderful and magical images that little girls create for that person second only to God. For most of my life, I struggled to understand why my father was not in my life. As a young child, I was only mildly aware that my family was different; that I was different because I did not have a traditional family structure. I was certainly aware that my father was not a part of my home, but his absence seemed natural because he had never been there. Clearly, if he had been there, I would have felt his absence, his distance and the hurt and pain associated with a loved one leaving. Because his 'leaving' was so early in my life, my pain was delayed. His absence really did not feel like a 'bad' thing for sometime; it was just my life.

It is very difficult if not impossible to decipher as a five or six year old what is "normal" and what is not. Even as adults, we are challenged by the concept. Are gay and lesbian issues such as same sex marriage normal? Is it normal for children to grow up in single parent households? What is normal? To answer these kinds of questions, we unconsciously refer to an internal set of qualifiers or filters to guide us. As children, however, we do not operate with a full set of tools to help decide where and how we fit in, what is normal, and what is not. We defer to our parents, our guardians, our teachers, and to our cultural and social dictates to steer us toward answers.

In my childhood, I referred to the systems, values, and beliefs established by my mother, grandmother, and my extended family. I felt a particularly strong connection to my grandmother, as a very young child because she was the primary caregiver when my mother was working. We lived with my grandmother from as early a time as I can remember until my mother married my brother's father when I was four or five years of age. We moved to southwest Detroit but still spent a significant amount of time with my grandmother because we attended the school in her neighborhood. From this marriage, my two brothers were born, Georgie (George) and Marcus. Georgie, named after his father, died of crib death when he was several months old. Marcus was born a year later in 1963. Because this relationship was not successful, we were again living with my grandmother shortly after Marcus was born.

In spite of the challenges we faced during this period, we always felt happy. Somehow, my mother was able to isolate us from the turmoil in her life. My childhood was a wonderful time filled with family activities, friends, lots of toys and dolls, and plenty of attention and guidance. I felt loved and very secure with only age appropriate issues to deal with. As a young child, if there were any major problems in the household, my sister and brother and I never knew of them. My most significant concern each day was finding the missing blue jack to complete my set of 10, trying to figure out why the string protruding from Chatty Cathy's back would not retract as it always did or reattaching my red ball to the elastic string of my 'bat & ball' with a toothpick so I could participate in the "Bat & Ball Tournament" my sister organized. She was good at that too!

My mother and grandmother constructed a very sheltered and loving atmosphere that made my sister and brother and I feel loved. We grew up in a very disciplined environment where we were rewarded and recognized for good behavior and punished when we chose to perform in ways that were unacceptable. Pretty normal to me! As one of thirteen grandchildren on the maternal side of my family, I had only ten cousins in my extended family. Fortunately, most were girls within a five-year age range, so we had quite a bit in common. One of the distinct aspects of my life at the time was the recognition that all of my cousins had fathers in their lives. Of the eight children born to Gammy and my grandfather, six married and produced thirteen children, including my sister, my bother and me, by the early 1960's.

My mother was the only one of her siblings with children who had no participation from the father of the children. Although I noticed that my cousins had fathers when I visited their homes or when we attended family gatherings, I was too young to fully process the relationships and to understand the full cast of characters and roles that mothers and fathers played. They were just my family. I did not separate them into husbands and wives with unique family structures of their own. They were just the adults in my family who were related to me. While I recognized the absence of my father and the presence of the their fathers, I was still too young to put it all together and really 'feel' and massage his absence, the absence of the 'father-daughter' connection and its ultimate potential to influence my life.

Within the confines of our close family, I was protected. I did not feel the indelible impression of fatherlessness on my spirit except for the occasional disappointments of my father's broken promises from which I recovered very quickly. It was not until I stepped outside of my immediate family structure that my uniqueness began to seep into my consciousness. School was the first real external indicator of my fatherlessness. For the first time, I felt unlike the other children. In elementary school, I can recall my homeroom teacher discussing an upcoming parent-teacher conference and the importance of having both parents attend the function. Of course, I was immediately alarmed because I had only one parent in my life. 'How would I handle this?' I thought. 'What would I tell my mother?' What would I tell my teacher if she asked why my father did not attend?' Maybe, she will not notice when my mother comes alone, I thought. Maybe, she will assume that my father was working and unable to attend.

School, through books, again broadened my perspective of family life by formalizing the concept of a traditional structure. I remember reading stories in the early grades where fathers played a prominent role in a family story. Remember the Dick and Jane stories? There was always a mother <u>and </u>a father in the story.

I recall participating in a musical production at Sampson Elementary School in the winter of 1967, where I sang the popular song, "Up, Up and Away", by the Fifth Dimension. My music teacher, Mrs. Dowdell, was my favorite teacher and was always so nice to me. I was so impressed by her because she had such a 'big' personality in addition to a 'booming' singing voice. When she asked me to sing the lead in the song, I immediately said no, because I knew I would not get up in front of 200 people to do anything. She was having none of it. She insisted that I sing and we set out to practice. We practiced first after class when it was just she and I. She then called upon me to practice during class. I turned inside out the first time she made this request! I did as asked and found that singing in front of others wasn't so bad. She continued to encourage me, making me believe that I could perform this insurmountable feat. I was upset at first but eventually came around and accepted the idea that I could take on those two hundred people in a heartbeat. I also found comfort in learning that my sister Debra was going for a part in the dance troop on the same program so I felt even better about it.

By the evening of the show, Debra was an expert in Mrs. Loving's well-choreographed tap dance number, "*Wade in the Water*" by Ramsey Lewis. Between her constant tapping and my imitation of Marilyn McCoo, my mother and grandmother had surely heard and seen enough. I was outfitted in my Christmas dress, a little black velvet number with an ivory-laced bodice, a cameo at the neckline and a hot pink satin sash at the waist. I thought I was all that and bag of chips too. I had no idea that I looked like a little Victorian schoolmarm with skinny legs, but I sang my heart out. I remember looking out into the audience to see my mother and grandmother and feeling so proud that they were there.

The following day, Mrs. Dowdell asked how my parents enjoyed the show. I was embarrassed to tell her that my mother and grandmother enjoyed the show very much because I had no father. I did not want her to know. I simply told her 'they' enjoyed the show very much.

The opportunity to participate in the program and to sing the lead was a life-changing event for me. I had been painfully shy and always afraid to assert myself. I recognized through this experience that I did have the courage to step forward to be seen and heard. I had something to give. I did something independent of my sister and it felt great! Years later, I saw Mrs. Dowdell at a restaurant and thanked her for the experience. She remembered me as a shy and reserved little girl who just needed a little push.

The popular media through television and movies also pricked my awareness of my fatherless condition. My sister and I grew up in the early sixties watching reruns of old Shirley Temple movies, a Sunday afternoon treat that we looked forward to experiencing. We could not wait to get home from church to see *Bill Kennedy's ShowTime*, a weekly television show featuring old movies. I can remember sitting in church at Hartford Avenue Baptist Church, and squirming restlessly while Reverend Charles Hill preached. I usually had no idea what he was talking about because I had a singular focus to get through the service and out of there so that I could get home and watch the Shirley Temple movie while my grandmother prepared dinner. Church was certainly not optional so I had to stick it out! Shirley Temple movies were a favorite for Bill Kennedy who loved to embellish the feature film for the day with anecdotes and trivia.

Every little girl of that era, black, white or otherwise adored Shirley Temple and wanted to be just like her although her movie career had begun some thirty years earlier. She represented for many the perfect little girl that everyone wanted to love. Shirley Temple was the ultimate "Daddy's Little Girl". My mother and grandmother probably wished Shirley Temple 'to disappear' because, of course, we wanted to look like her with her trademark 'Shirley Temple curls'. We did not just want the curls on special occasions; we wanted them all the time. My mother and grand-mother were not having it because only they had a clue as to the effort that was required to make it happen.

First, we were black and Shirley was white. There were no

black children on television during this era to mimic. Shirley's hair was at least naturally straight to begin with and then it was curled. The process to transform our hair took forever! Not completely straight, our hair was soft and straighter than most of our peers. We had so called 'good hair', which was not always a good thing for us. Unfortunately, in school, it often set us apart from the other girls who thought that we thought we were cute or somehow better, an interesting form of prejudice within racial boundaries. Even with 'good hair', it was nothing short of a formidable task to create Shirley Temple curls. I always got my hair done first because as Tina Turner would say, my hair was 'nice and easy'. My grandmother would wash my hair in the bathtub and roll it up wet with what seemed like a thousand of the homemade rollers created from hairpins wrapped in paper strips torn from brown paper bags – ghetto rollers. The following morning I was cute! I was even cuter than Shirley Temple and had curls for a week. My sister, on the other hand, had hair that was longer than my hair but a little 'rough' as Ms. Turner would say. Her hair had to be washed, pressed with a warm comb, and then adorned with the same lovely ghetto rollers. At the end of the day, we were happy campers because we had shoulder length bouncy Shirley Temple curls.

We watched every feature film in which Shirley Temple starred, from *Little Miss Marker* made in 1934 to *A Kiss for Corliss* made in 1949. Her movies were wonderful because there was always a happy conclusion where good triumphed over evil. She was always rescued just in time from harms way. I was particularly drawn to those films where her character reunited with or was 'saved' by her father or father figure. In the movie *The Little Princess*, Shirley portrays Sara, the pampered daughter of a British officer. Left in boarding school when her father goes off to war, Sara's world is turned upside down when he is reported dead. Destitute, Sara is made a servant at the school, yet she refuses to let her spirit be broken. She also refuses to believe her father is gone and begins searching the army hospitals to find him. She finds him, he professes his love and devotion to her, and they live happily ever after.

In the film, *Heidi*, she portrays the spirited young heroine of the popular children's novel. In the film, an aunt who tires of the job of raising the orphaned Heidi takes her into the Swiss Mountains to live with her gruff grandfather, a hermit who comes to adore and care for her. The aunt later returns to steal Heidi away and sells her to a family whose invalid daughter needs a companion. Bullied by an evil governess, Heidi still charms the entire household and never stops trying to return to her beloved grandfather. She is finally reunited with her grandfather and again lives happily ever after with him.

In *Poor Little Rich Girl,* Shirley's character, Little Barbara gets lost and is then picked up by entertainers who make her part of their act. Barbara's father hears the act on the radio and finds his lost daughter. They are reunited and live happily ever after, one more time.

Through the eyes and heart of a seven-year-old, I saw a little girl constantly looking to a father or father-like figure for rescue, reassurance, and guidance. I saw the loving relationship and the wonderful bond that her character seemed to have with the male figures. In most of her movies, there was a male figure there to make everything all right in the end. She seemed to have the 'Daddy's Little Girl' thing down to a science and was eventually always loved, always protected and always happy in the end. Wasn't that the way life was supposed to be? Weren't all little girls supposed to have loving fathers to adore them?

Adore. What a wonderful word. Interesting enough, when I checked the Webster website to get a definition for adore, I found the following: *'to regard with loving admiration and devotion <adored his daughter>!'* Even Webster gets it, using <adored his daughter> as an example for word usage! I know my father would have adored me if he had given himself a chance to know me. I adored him or at least the image I had of him for a very long time.

Just after I began writing this book, while driving home from work one evening, I was struck by the words of a beautiful song entitled *Butterfly Kisses* by country western singer, Bob Carlisle. Mr. Carlisle describes his loving relationship with his daughter from her development as a young child wearing pigtails and ribbons, to her wedding day where she looked so much like her mother. The song's title, *Butterfly Kisses,* describes the delicate lashes of his baby daughter's eyes as they sweep across his cheek when she is held closely. As I listened, I found myself in tears as the amorous words pulled at my heartstrings and touched the deep-seated delicate wounds whose existence I was just beginning to discover. At the age of forty, I was again feeling the pain of fatherlessness. The lyrics beautifully describe several precious moments unique to a father and daughter. Even the 'daddy's little girl' theme is used in the song:

There's two things I know for sure.

She was sent here from heaven, and she's daddy's little girl.

As I drop to my knees by her bed at night, she talks to Jesus, and I close my eyes.

And I thank God for all the joy in my life,

Oh, but most of all, for...

Butterfly kisses after bedtime prayer...

I immediately began to think about how fortunate his daughter was to have such a loving father. What a beautiful gift to be loved in this way! Why did I have a father who was not able to love me at all? Why did he not want to know my sister or me? How could he have just walked away? Where does a man find the capacity to abandon the product of his loins? Why me? Why? Didn't I deserve more? How could one man feel so intensely for his daughter and another man feel nothing? I felt stunned and frozen by my own grief.

I thought of my boys as I struggled to find the answers to my questions. I immediately felt engulfed with love for them. I thought of how much I love being a mother and all of the joy and the challenges that accompany the journey; a journey and opportunity that I would trade for nothing. I thought of how privileged I was to have the opportunity to create and guide a human life. The opportunity to lay the spiritual foundation for their lives; to provide them the emotional support and nurturing to architect their self-esteem; to teach them to work for what they want in life and to love and respect others. I felt blessed just to have the chance to experience their lives as a subset of my own. I cannot imagine my life without them. I cannot imagine walking away from them. What or who could be more important in this world than to nurture and guide my sons?

I have achieved success in practically every aspect of my life. I worked hard to attain my undergraduate degree while often working full time to help support my family. I also worked hard to achieve my MBA attending school at night while working full time with two small children, a feat not possible without a supportive husband and a man who is the true definition of a father. I have worked hard to reach a level in my life where I can take care of my children and myself. I've done well in every job assignment, exceeding expectations when often less was expected. I've lived my dream to become an entrepreneur. I tried hard to be a good daughter to my mother particularly through her illness and her transition in 1990 to breast cancer at the young age of fifty-three. Nothing, however, has been as rewarding an experience as motherhood. The experience to mold and develop a life is a God-given opportunity and one that should be favored over all other life goals and aspirations if it is freely chosen.

I once read a quote by Jacqueline Kennedy Onassis in a

popular woman's magazine that I thought was so very profound. When asked what her greatest life achievement had been, she indicated that it had been raising her two children, Caroline and John, to become grounded and productive adults. This is what being a parent is all about. Here is a woman who lived a life of privilege and opportunity, traveled the world, lived as the wife of an American president, married a tycoon and so much more. Yet, when all is said and done, the most basic and innate aspect of her life, the one born out of natural instinct, motherhood and raising her children, rose to the top as her foundation for true achievement and happiness.

These feelings are not gender specific. Most fathers love their children as much as mothers and hold the role they play in their children's lives in as high esteem as do their female counterparts. Nevertheless, what has happened to our *black* fathers? Where are they?

Statistics say that black fathers are missing in action in epidemic proportions. In large urban areas like Detroit, sixty percent of black children are born into single-family homes where the father is not present. What is key about this statement is the reality that these children are 'born' into single family homes. The horse is before the cart because their parents are not only not married as the children are born, but the ultimately never marry.

Do not get me wrong; many black fathers are active participants in their children's lives. They are the quintessential fathers. However, far too many black males make babies and do not follow through to become fathers. They simply become 'babies daddies' or sperm donors and never function as fathers.

This writing is not intended to indict black men or black fatherhood. Black men are good and black men are good fathers. I watched, as a child, the warm and loving relationships that my female cousins and friends had with their fathers. I've seen many fictional accounts of black fathers in countless television shows, movies, advertisements, etc. My most significant knowledge and experience however have come from watching the beautiful relationship that my boys have with their father. Simply put, he is a great black father. There is nothing fancy about his approach; he is simply there for their every need because he loves them. He did not attend classes or workshops to learn to be a good father. He didn't have to be taught. His stature as a good father comes simply from his love for his boys and his desire to nurture and guide them.

There are many other examples of extraordinary black fathers in our communities. Radio show host Tom Joyner has a weekly segment called 'Real Fathers, Real Men', an outstanding and informative segment highlighting the magnificent achievements of the black father. The stories are compelling because black daughters and sons, wives, granddaughters and grandsons, voice them with such compassion and love. The segment raises the awareness that black fathers DO play a critical role in the lives of the daughters and women they touch. It is a unique and unprecedented format in which to voice the hearts and soles of black fathers. Still, all too often, black fathers are still not there.

Another interesting trend is the apparent change in the attitude toward the relationship between child bearing and marriage. There was a time when bearing a child outside of wedlock was certainly an unacceptable condition that was hidden or camouflaged. Today, many young black women wear their "out-of-wedlock" pregnancy as a badge of honor. According to *Newsweek Magazine, August 30, 1993,* this widening gap between the concept of marriage and child bearing has changed significantly over the last 40 years:

For blacks, the institution of marriage has been devastated in the last generation: 2 out of 3 first births to black women under 35 are now out of wedlock. In 1960, the number was 2 out of 5. It is not likely to improve any time soon. A black child born today has only a 1-in-5 chance of growing up with two parents until the age of 16, according to University of Wisconsin demographer Larry L. Bumpass. The impact, of course, is not only on black families but also on all of society. Fatherless homes boost crime rates, lower educational attainment and add dramatically to the welfare rolls.

Many black leaders rush to portray out-of-wedlock birth as solely a problem of an entrenched underclass. It is not. It cuts across economic lines. Among the poor, a staggering 65 percent of never-married black women have children, double the number for whites. Even among the well to do, the differences are striking: 22 percent of never-married black women with incomes above $75,000 have children, almost 10 times as many as whites.

For many black women, the problem is an economic or underclass issue as described by Newsweek Magazine, August 30, 1993:

In every economic group, black women are two to seven times more likely to have a child before marriage than white women. The percent of never-married women ages 15 to 44 who have children:

	Black	**White**
Under $10,000	66%	32%
$10,000-$20,000	50%	19%
$25,000-$30,000	32%	8%
$30,000-$35,000	34%	7%
$50,000-$75,000	11%	3%
Over 75,000	22%	3%

There is clearly a trend in play that can be postulated any number of ways, but at the end of the day, there continues to be a significant number of African American children born out of wedlock and into environments where their fathers do not partici-pate. This trend and its relationship to lower income levels make the "out-of-wedlock" and fatherlessness concepts a reality that is even more difficult to address. Even though teen pregnancy rates have declined over the last decade, African American teens continue to have children at alarming rates. According to the National Center for Health Statistics, despite the overall decline, young women of color are disproportionately affected by teenage pregnancy. In 2000, the birth rates for African American teenagers were reported as the lowest ever in the 40 years for which data for African American women are available:

- In 1997, 7.7 per 1,000 African American women under the age of 15 became pregnant compared with 11.8 per 1,000 in 1990

- In 1997, 119.8 per 1,000 African American women 15 to 17 years of age became pregnant compared with 165 per 1,000 in 1990

- In 1997, 248 per 1,000 African American women 18 to 19 years of age became pregnant compared with 295.3 per 1,000 in 1990

- From 1991 to 2000, birth rates for Mexican, Puerto Rican, Cuban, and "other" Hispanic teenagers fell by 6 to 13 percent each, while rates for American Indian and Asian Pacific Islander teenagers fell 20 to 21 percent, rates for non-Hispanic White teens fell 24 percent, and rates for African American teenagers fell 31 percent. The rate for African American teenagers in 2000 is an historic low (data available since 1960)

- In 2000, the birth rate for African American women 10 to 14 years of age was 2.4 per 1,000 compared with 4.9 per 1,000 in 1990

- In 2000, the birth rate for African American women 15 to 17 years of age was 50.4 per 1,000 compared with 82.3 per 1,000 in 1990

- In 2000, the birth rate for African American women 18 to 19 years of age was 121.3 per 1,000 compared with 152.9 per 1,000 in 1990

The impact of fatherlessness resulting from teen pregnancy or otherwise is significant. The data from the National Center for Health Statistics also indicates that:

- 94 percent of teens believe that if they were involved in a pregnancy they would stay in school; in reality, 70 percent eventually complete high school

- 51 percent of teens believe that if they were involved in a pregnancy they would marry the mother/father; in reality, 81 percent of teenage births are to unmarried teens

- 26 percent of teens believe that they would need welfare to support a child; in reality 56 percent receive public assistance to cover the cost of delivery and 25 percent of teen mothers receive public assistance by their early twenties

This data suggest that 30% of those teens who become pregnant do not complete high school and are therefore challenged when they enter the job market. With no job skills because of their youth and the lack of a high school education, they are unable to attain employment that will sustain themselves and their children. With an astounding 81% of these teenagers who will not marry the fathers of their babies, they are further disadvantaged to participate in the economic and social system, as they must develop childcare alternatives on their own, support themselves and their children, all when they are hardly mature enough to handle the responsibilities inherent in parenthood. It is not surprising that a significant number of these teenage mothers who are without the support of their families and the fathers of their babies turn to public assistance and begin or perpetuate the cycle of fatherlessness for their children.

Additionally, according to long-term studies in the United States, girls who grow up without their fathers are more at risk of becoming pregnant while still teenagers. The studies indicate that the absence of biological fathers from the home is the most significant factor for teenage pregnancy. The studies revealed that the earlier a father left, the greater the risk of teenage pregnancy. Rates increased from about one in twenty for girls whose fathers were present, to one in three for girls whose father left early in their lives. Early absence was defined as the first five years of a girl's life. The studies suggest that the possible explanations included the exposure of fatherless girls to their mothers' dating behavior, or the girls undergoing personality changes that drive them towards early and unstable bonds with men.

How had my life been impacted by fatherlessness? Had my personality and expectations been shaped by my past? Was my template for male-female relationships flawed? Reaching forty years of age was a very stimulating and introspective time in my life. I had for the first time truly begun to look back, take stock of my life, and question my future direction. Feeling as if I was half way through my life, I needed to understand what was important to me so that I could begin to plan and develop strategies to move my life forward in the direction that I desired. All of a sudden, I found myself on the side of life that really required me to think about the rest of my life. Prior to forty, I floated along through some aspects of my life with a short-term perspective or vision of my existence, letting things happen to me when I had the ability to be proactive instead of reactive. Getting older was always something that did not refer to me. I was young and did not need to think long-term. However, I was always willing to examine the idea when the time came. Even though these thoughts were not conscience, they were nonetheless reality in that my behaviors voiced them loudly. Don't get me wrong, I had not wandered through my life aimlessly, but looking back I saw several areas where I could have made better decisions had I taken the time to see the big picture instead of focusing upon those influences staring me in the face at the time.

With the 'rest of my life' voice shouting, "where are we going?" I knew I needed to get moving. One of the first things I recognized was that I was simply glad to be alive. I had been blessed with 40 years of good health with little more than the typical cold or flu and pregnancy related ailments. Nonetheless, my most significant health fear has and continues to be breast cancer. Seven years earlier, I lost my mother to the disease that was discovered when she was forty-nine years of age. After a reoccurrence of the cancer four years later in 1990, she lost her battle. Would I have to incorporate cancer into my plan? Could I be my mother in nine short years? I am now at the age of forty-nine, taking my health seriously, not waiting until something occurs to 'start' exercising and improving my diet. I have a personal trainer who has outlined a program to roll back or slow the aging process. I now watch my diet closely and consider the benefit or value of everything that I put in my mouth. It is definite change in the process called life. Today, I celebrate each of my birthdays as if it is my last. I will tell anyone my age because I am glad to be and content that I have had the privilege to be a citizen of the world for forty-nine years.

In my self-examination, I am thankful to have a great career and thankful to have two wonderful boys at the center of my life. I completed my bachelor's degree in Business Administration in 1981 and my MBA in 1993. I have worked hard in my career to earn a good salary and make a comfortable life for my boys and myself.

While feeling mostly content with these aspects of my life, my personal life was in shambles. I was separated from my husband of 19 years for a three-year period and struggling mightily to find a comfort zone. I had not realized how difficult it would be to step out of a long-term marriage and into this 'something else', that is not a traditional societal unit. Although the decision to leave my marriage had been mine, I was unprepared for the considerable emotional turmoil that I experienced and imposed on others. My actions hurt my husband, my children, my family, and me. I was completely out of sorts and needed badly to understand why I was off balance. I was not accustomed to failure. If this was the right thing to do, why did it hurt so badly? Why was it so hard to experience? I had prevailed at everything in my life that I pursued up to this point. I knew I needed to take inventory and to analyze the data to structure a future that would be emotionally balanced not only for myself but also more importantly for my children. How would I ensure that the decision to end my marriage with their dad did not have a negative impact on them as perhaps my father's decision to walk away had imposed upon me?

I decided to compartmentalize these and other challenge areas to better organize my struggle, and attack each one individually. I realized that I needed to examine and understand my past before I could move forward to build a life with any semblance of peace and balance. I understood where I was standing, but I suspected that where I stood was influenced by my past. I asked myself several questions. Why did my marriage fail? What role did my up-bringing play in its failure? I know that I was at least fifty percent responsible. I always behaved very independently, feeling the need to be in control, however never in a pushy or negative manner. What was that all about? Was I pushing for my place at the front of the line because I had always stood in the background as a child? Was I afraid to depend

completely on a man as I had seen my mother do unsuccess-
fully? What role did growing up without a father play in the
events of my life and my 'independent' spirit? Did my experience
paint my view of love, marriage, relationships and security and
trust? Where was my template?

To find answers to these and other questions, I began to
search bookstores and the Internet for information on the father-
daughter relationship. For most of my life, I recognized that I was
without a father and had been very interested in that special
relationship that I did not have. I believed there was a link between the failure of my marriage and the way I viewed male-
female relationships and my wisdom related to fatherlessness. I
needed to do a reality check, to see what the rest of the world
thought about female fatherlessness, particularly black females. I
found a fair amount of information about like gender relationships
between parents and children, i.e., fathers and sons and mothers
and daughters. I found very little about fathers and daughters or
mothers and sons and even less about black or African American
fatherlessness and the impact of their daughters. Clearly, this is
a unique and vastly under-studied topic.

It is for this reason that I am compelled to tell this story. I
know that I am not alone in my experience. I know that other
black women with similar experiences have some of the same
questions and have experienced the same pain and confusion.
There are countless other women who carry with them a deep
seated pain that oozes out with the lyrics of a certain song, or at

the mere site of a father holding his daughter. It is a hurt that can not be quantified or measured; it is without scale. There are many young fatherless black females who are not yet mature enough to understand the circumstances of their lives and the future challenges they may face.

My story may facilitate others, who like me, live the experience and struggle to understand why they are who they are. I want black women to examine their options and to move forward to make better choices so that their daughters do not suffer the same circumstance. I want those fathers or those contemplating fatherhood to understand the critical role they play in the lives of their daughters and the tremendous responsibility they have to perform their paternal role. I want those fathers who are not with their daughters or their sons to reconnect and recognize that the cost to remain disconnected is higher than they can comprehend.

I know there are many black women who share my feelings. There is that 'something' in their lives that is missing. They live with the same quiet anger and confusion that is systemically woven into the fabric of my life. There are millions of African American fatherless women who have experienced the loneliness and heartbreak of a father who has been physically and/or emotionally absent. As a child, absence did in fact make the heart grow fonder, as the old cliché suggests. However, as I matured into adulthood, my heart was no longer the gale wind that directed my sail. I began to ask why and to seek answers to comfort my soul as my deeply imbedded wounds awaken. I began to appreciate my mother more.

It was evident by the life pattern my father established that he was 'a rolling stone', hence the title of the book. He probably never planned to have children in his relationships, but took no responsible measures for prevention. My father simply moved from one center of pleasure to the next, wreaking havoc as he invaded one life after another, creating one life after another. Papa was a rolling stone.

I again stepped back to examine whether the personal issues I had begun to raise were in fact significant or real enough to have the impact that I was suggesting. Was I over rating this whole fatherlessness issue? Was I over reacting? One evening during the very early stages of writing this book, I was drawn to a television news story about actor Christopher Reeves and others like him with spinal cord injuries. The segment featured the recent bio-technical advances developed to provide increased mobility for those with severe spinal cord injuries. As I watched, I felt saddened by the significant physical limitations these individuals faced in their daily lives. I could not image the emotional suffering that surely accompanied their physical challenges.

Just prior to the segment, I was feeling a little 'down' as I searched my mind for possible reasons why my father just left and never returned. As I watched the program, I began to compare my fatherlessness issue with the enormous health obstacles faced by these spinal cord patients and resolved very quickly that my 'stuff' was nothing by comparison. My mind and body were certainly in full working condition. I could depend only upon myself to get up and move about, to provide for my most basic needs without intervention from others. What was I crying about? I felt discouraged and began to question my motive for writing this book. I stopped writing for the evening. Several years later in 2005, Christopher Reeve would die.

As I lay in bed later that night, I began to think about my life choices and my effort to raise my boys to be productive citizens who will respect the family unit and the critical role they could play as fathers. Fortunately, my boys have good role models. I regained my focus by rejoicing in the favorable outcomes to my choices and the positive impression that these choices have had on my boys. I did select a good father for them. As I tossed and turned, the deep dark hole inside of me began to make its way to the surface, reopening and pouring out all of the feelings generated by a legacy of fatherlessness. I held and caressed the missed opportunities, the feelings of being unloved by my father, the pain of rejection and abandonment, and the enormous sense of anger and resentment toward my father. I held on to these sensitivities like I was holding on to a lover. I did not want to let them go because somehow the pain was comforting. I had a right to the pain. I had a battle that I needed to fight. I had something of my father to hold on to, even if it was a heart full of pain. I took ownership of the pain because it linked me to him. I cried myself to sleep.

With the rise of the morning sun, I awakened with a sense of peace. With a clearer mind, I closed the break in my heart and let go of, at least temporarily, the pain of the night before. As I lay in bed, I began to realize that while the pain was certainly a driver for me to tell my story, it should not be as significant a force as I had perhaps allowed it to become. I needed to find a way to be productive with the pain. I needed the pain to navigate a path that would allow me to accept my father 'as is' and perhaps to a final destination of forgiveness.

With this revelation, I felt renewed in my desire to tell my story so that other women, particularly black women would begin to understand how important it is to make intelligent choices in the men who will father our children. Their little girls should not grow up as I did without their fathers. I wanted to tell my story to young black men so that they too would be equipped with the awareness of the enormous responsibility that they have in fathering children, particularly their daughters. Their daughters too should not grow up without the presence of their fathers as role models for their future relationships. Clearly, we make better or more informed choices when we have had the opportunity to model our behaviors after those who demonstrate acceptable behaviors. Without fathers in our lives, good fathers, we have either no role models or poor role models by which to guide our decisions and behaviors.

With the increasing number of fatherless homes among black households, it is no wonder that as black women, we make poor choices in selecting our mates. We don't know what to look for. By default, we end up falling head over heels in love with the first guy to tell us we're pretty or fine or hot. We have no criteria other than 'he likes me and he pays attention to me' so he must love me. We all know adult women who accept a sexual relationship as a trade off for love.

I have spent most of my adult life trying to please others, particularly the men in my life. I have always sought their approval, always trying to understand and meet their criteria. What about my criteria? My experience taught little about selection criteria. I surely understood the basics of male-female relationships but I lacked a good model or road map by which to plot my strategy for selection. I did know that I did not want a man like my father.

I decided that evening that while the scars of abandonment and fatherlessness might not be visible and certainly not physically debilitating by comparison to spinal cord injuries; the scars were in fact daunting and did have the potential to be emotionally disabling. The great thing about life is that we can learn from the mistakes of others.

I chose a good man to father my children. My awareness of this was peaked by the development of my own nuclear family, after my boys were born in 1982 and 1985. Without much intent by my husband or me, our boys learned to understand and to depend upon our differing gender based roles. My boys believed their Dad to be the strongest man on earth and able to protect the family from all harm. They trusted him implicitly. They were convinced that he was super human like their heroes, Superman and Spider man. When they were four and seven years of age, respectively, their Dad upon returning home from a business trip in California showed them a shark's tooth that he had purchased from a gift shop. He convinced the boys, rather easily I might add, that he had wrestled a shark in the ocean and removed its tooth as a symbol of triumph. Their eyes lit up like candles when they heard the story. They did not doubt their Dad for a second. They were all in.

Children believe that their fathers represent strength and valor. To a child, a father is everything: someone to love, to look up to, and to follow. A year later, General Motors transferred their Dad to Spring Hill, Tennessee for a six-month assignment to work as an engineer on the Saturn project. He was gone for a ten-day stretch at a time, returning only every other weekend. The very first night that he was gone, my older son, then seven years old, began wetting the bed. He had been fully potty trained by the age of three and was not wetting the bed prior to his Dad's new assignment. When I asked him what was going on that prevented him from getting up to go to the bathroom, he told me that he was afraid that a bad guy would get him because his Dad was gone. He absolutely refused to get up in the night to go to the bathroom and as a result, he wet the bed every single night.

I have always wanted to be 'Daddy's Little Girl'. I have always carried with me this fairy tale or mythical vision of a father-daughter relationship. When I think of my father and the role I imagined him to play in my life, I think of the beautiful poem "Footprints". I imagined it was my father walking alongside of me as I navigated life's journeys, as did my sons' father. I imagined that my father was there to guide me at my weakest points and to be there to carry me when I cannot go it alone. I imagined him to be my night and shining armor.

There are times when I feel so vulnerable to my life's circumstance. Something as simple as a song playing on the radio can wipe me completely out, changing my mood for the balance of the day. Sometimes, that mood change is a good, particularly when I can recognize that the 'glass is half full'. On those days, I think of my mother and the love that I feel for her, 16 years after her death. I smile when I think of how successful she was in raising three children to be productive adults, all with a college education and meaningful careers. I know that she is proud of us. She stuck around to endure the pain and challenge of abandonment, raising us without the benefit of our father's presence or financial support. Sure, she had help from her parents, because she came from a loving family and a community who refused to let her fail. I rejoice in the values that my mother and grandmother established for me. My sister and brother and I were taught to be independent above all else. I can still hear my mother's direction regarding independence and men.

"Don't position yourself to depend on a man or anyone else", she would say. "Get your education and take care of yourself".

We were drilled with this wisdom throughout our teenage years. My mother was so threatened by the concept that we might be sexually active as teenagers that she demanded we take birth control pills. We would make it a regular practice to drop a pill a day into the toilet because we suspected that she might be checking the medicine cabinet to make sure we were taking the pills. I understand today as I understood then that she wanted only to eliminate the possibility that we might become pregnant and not complete our education, which would ultimately lead to a life of dependency.

When we began to date, she would tell us "Don't fool around with those boys and get pregnant! If you come home pregnant, I'll kill you!"

She got my attention. I would pretend to ignore the threat but always took it seriously. I knew that she would not harm me if I did become pregnant, but I understood that pregnancy would change my life dramatically. I was not prepared to take on that challenge or to risk her wrath. She was very strict and in control of what I did, and who I befriended. While she rarely focused on homework, she was very clear about her expectations when the report card arrived. Nothing less than a 'B" was acceptable. I was allowed to attend school related functions that were held at the school, but not allowed to attend parties and functions hosted by students in their homes or at party halls.

Even upon graduation from high school, I was only allowed to date or see my boyfriend one day out of the weekend. If I saw him on Friday, I couldn't see him on Saturday or Sunday. I was not allowed to 'date' whenever I wanted until I was twenty years old. I can remember thinking that my mother was so mean and unreasonable. I did not understand until much later that her motive was protection. She wanted badly to shield my sister and I from the multitude of opportunities for poor choice. She wanted us to avoid the temptation of drugs, the allure of sex, and the enticement of alcohol.

While I always tried to listen to my mother, I did feel that her analysis of men was a little harsh. Her words were clearly a product of her experience. She unfortunately positioned herself to depend on the men in her life to sustain her emotionally and to some degree financially. She grew up in a family where her father took care of the entire family of a wife and eight children and did so very well. This was all she knew. Her upbringing influenced the expectations that she had for her relationships. I know now that she only sought to protect my sister, brother and I, even if her methods were a little aggressive.

When my mood change moves in the other direction, I experience the 'glass is half empty' syndrome, feeling a strong sense of loss for what I perceive my loss to be as well as the hardships that I know my mother endured. I feel sorry that she had to struggle as she did to take care of us alone. Because my father visited the neighborhood often, I am sure she watched or was aware of his life free of the responsibility of children and fatherhood. He was emancipated to live and 'roll' as he pleased, committing neither himself nor his financial resources to assist in raising us. I feel sorry that her life was at times difficult, even if some of her challenges resulted from her own decisions. I grieve for the unhappiness, the pain, and fear that I know she felt when she peered into her future and saw nothing but one challenge after another. She deserved better than that.

I feel sorry for myself when I think of all that my father took from me. I think about all of my paternal aunts and uncles and the little exposure that I have had to them. They are all wonderful people with good hearts and bountiful spirits who would have contributed significantly to my life. I think about all of my cousins who lived in the same city, blocks away that I never had an opportunity to cultivate a relationship with as I did with the relatives on my mother's side. I grieve the family relationships that never happened.

I think about the 'Daddy's Little Girl' concept and the fairly tale vision that I never got a chance to live with my father. I never got the opportunity to make him larger than life, to look up to him, or to admire him. I never got the opportunity to look to him for advice and guidance. I think about the many ways that I must be like him but have no awareness of our likeness because I knew so little of him. I am heart sick that my father lived within 5 to 20 miles of me for my entire life, yet he chose not to participate in my life. The only picture I have of my father is the picture on his obituary.

I wanted my father to love me. I needed my father to love me. I wanted to feel special in only the way that a little girl can feel special to her father. I wanted to call him 'Daddy' and mean it from the bottom of my heart. I wanted to sit on his knee when I was troubled or hurt and hear him say that everything was going to be ok. I would have trusted his every word as I listened to his sharp masculine voice and watched his handsome face as he spoke. I wanted my father to give me away at my wedding. I wanted him to look into the eyes of my husband and speak the unspoken message that he had better take care of *his* daughter. I wanted him to be a grandfather to my boys. He surely missed their first steps as he missed mine. I wanted to be a part of his family as well as be a part of my mother's family. I wanted to love him and I wanted him to love me. I wanted my father to have a home within my heart.

He was the first man that I wanted to love me. He did not. He would not.

Chapter Four – You Broke Your Promise & Let Go of My Hand

"Fathers teach children how to stand, first by holding their hand, and then by letting go." — Author Unknown

When we are born into the world, we are more often than not, born with a natural connection to two people, our biological parents. The child-parent biological connection is synonymous to links in a chain where a 'child', a weak and vulnerable link, has a single connection at each side; a mother link bringing all of her gender specific maternal tenderness and strength and a father link with his construct for love, guidance and affirmation. We have seen the relationship depicted many times at the mall, at church, at a traffic light, or at a crowded outdoor festival where both mother and father hold a young child's hand with the child securely held in the center creating a connecting structure. The child is the center point, important and pivotal in relationship to their parents and rest of the world. Like links in a chain; a vision that speaks a thousand words.

Certainly, our world is not a perfect one. While birth and entry to this world is, at least, for a moment, a beautiful and perfect circumstance, it is not everyone's reality. As infants, we enter this world in a total state of dependence needing immediate care and attention. In far too many cases, there is only one parent, the mother, who is available to provide all that is needed. It is alarming that so many African American girls and women position themselves to be single mothers or a 'baby's mama. Where has the concept of a meaningful relationship and marriage gone? What has happened to the idea of requiring and getting respect for oneself? The bulk of the responsibility I believe lies with black women. The buck has to stop somewhere. Given the bulk of the responsibility and the significant hardship that many single mothers experience, it is reasonable that the instigation for change start here. As women, we too often do not choose to lie down with men who have shown us through other experiences that they are not responsible and do not want to be responsible for fathering a child. The message is simple. Do not lie down with them. Do not perpetuate the cycle and create a culture where your child has no father in his or her life in the same way that you perhaps did not have the presence of a father in your life. Instead, take the unique opportunity to teach, particularly the girls, through your behaviors that they are worthy of respect and deserve to be adored. As women, we have a responsibility to teach our girls and our boys about the virtues of family and the opportunity to create a model by which they can follow to conduct their lives as adults.

I recently read a particularly disconcerting article written by Joy Jones, a writer for the Washington Post, titled "Marriage is for White People". In the article, she speaks to a comment made by a 12-year-old elementary school student in Southeast Washington while teaching a career exploration class.

"I was pleasantly surprised when the boys in the class stated that being a good father was a very important goal to them, more meaningful than making money or having a fancy title". She goes on to respond by saying, "That's wonderful! I think I'll invite some couples in to talk about being married and rearing children."

"Oh, no," objected the student. "We're not interested in the part about marriage. Only about how to be good father."

Another child chimed in 'speaking as if the word left a nasty taste in his mouth' "Marriage is for white people."

Ms. Jones writes, "He's right, at least statistically. The marriage rate for African American has been dropping since the 1960s, and today, we have the lowest marriage rate of any racial group in the United States. In 2001, according to the U.S. Census, 43.3 percent of black men and 41.9 percent of black women in America had never been married, in contrast to 27.4 percent and 20.7 percent respectively for whites. African American women are the least likely in our society to marry. In the period between 1970 and 2001, the overall marriage rate in the United States declined by 17 percent; but for African Americans, it fell by 34 percent."

These statistics paint a very clear and dramatic message to young black children. They are witness and often the subject of the statistics. They see the pregnancy and subsequent birth and the child, but don't see the marriage as a part of the scenario. We are becoming or perhaps we are a society of 'baby mamas' and 'baby daddies'.

"Sex, love and childbearing have become a la carte choices rather than a package deal that comes with marriage." Ms. Jones writes.

This clearly signals a breakdown in what is the traditional idea of family. Most importantly, this pattern of behavior changes the male template from the head of the nuclear family to a 'baby's daddy' with no membership in the nuclear family and no responsibility. Far too many young men just walk away; modeling the behavior that they have witnessed and lived.

My father just walked away. My father did not want to be a father. He did not want the responsibility. Again, there is no crime in not wanting the responsibility of fatherhood. If this is the case, then 'don't lie down' without taking measures to prevent pregnancy or just 'don't lie down'. My father made the decision to lie down when he was not prepared emotionally or financially to be accountable. He came from a family that provided outstanding family role models.

My father made a conscious choice to walk away not just from his responsibility as a father but more importantly from the opportunity and joy of being my father; an experience that I am sure would have been an extraordinary and fulfilling journey. Having had the opportunity to look into the eyes of a new life, to feel the warmth and sweet smell of a baby's breath, I can't imagine what was powerful enough to pull him in another direction; a direction away from me. Did he move on to the next woman or relationship? Was it the nightlife that was so compelling? Was it his singing career that made having a family so unattractive? Was he really meandering through life so aimlessly and so unconsciously to the impact of his actions? Did he think about me when he walked away? Did he think so little of me that it was easy to leave or did he think of so little of himself that he felt that he had nothing to contribute? Why?

Had my father been around for the journey, he would have known that I was a sweet child and worthy to be adored. He would have known that my eyes lit up like diamonds when my grandmother called me 'sweet' as I helped her with the dishes. In his absence, he had no way of knowing that I clung to my grandmother as a surrogate parent, as his replacement. He had no way of knowing that I needed *his* attention, *his* acceptance, and *his* love.

He would have experienced as my grandmother and my mother did, my special need for attention. It was not that I felt unloved or unaccepted, but I needed the kind of attention that provided reassurance. I did not like to be scolded and took it very personally. If I thought that I might be rejected somehow or that someone would be angry with me, I would go the extra mile to be embraced. I never attempted to manipulate or deceive but I understood how to step back and to envision the 'bigger' picture and determine how to behave.

My relationship with my mother very early on was a bit of a challenge because of this need for reassurance. I did not understand that when she was not responsive to me because she had had a bad day at work that it was for that reason and had nothing to do with me. If she snapped at me because I awakened her from the nap she took each day after work, I took it personally. I would then find a way later in the day to do or say something nice to make up for it because I did not want her to be upset with me.

Where my sister was concerned, because she was 'always in charge', I would often feel snubbed or subordinate to her. If she were annoyed with me while in the company of our friends, she would urge them to exclude me from the game or the current activity. If I was not picked to be on the 'right' team or not picked at all, I was deeply offended. My favorite response to them was to storm away in a huff (but not in too much of a hurry) and say 'Nobody loves me, no one cares!' I wanted to punish them for mistreating me and I felt that this was the way to get to them. If I rushed off too quickly, then I wouldn't be around to hear them recant. Well, recant they did not. In fact, they proceeded to 'cant' even further, laughing and teasing as I walked away. I think I entertained them more than I appealed to their character or conscience. What they did not know and what they were too young to interpret was my need to belong and the need to feel affirmed in that belonging. Had my father been in my life, would my need to belong have been so strong?

I didn't get to pick the most important man in my life. Four years his junior and a senior in high school, my mother first met my father in the neighborhood. My father had grown up in the neighborhood on 21st street; however, he attended a different elementary and middle school than my mother. Many years ago when I asked my mother how she met my father, she spoke very endearingly about seeing him in the neighborhood as he visited his older brother who lived also on Woodrow Street, but several blocks down.

In the same neighborhood, my grandfather, and my father's older brothers ran the family owned business, the Wright Printing Company. My father was the youngest of eleven children from a hard working religious family of entrepreneurs. My grandfather, prior to moving his family to Detroit, operated a print shop in Hannibal, Missouri and published a weekly newspaper, the Hannibal Register. With such strong roots in the neighborhood, it was not unusual to see my father out and about.

When my mother and her girl friends were old enough to frequent the popular neighborhood concert hall and nightspot called the 20 Grand, they were there and guess who was featured! Charles William Wright! With a voice as smooth as Billy Eckstine and a stage presence and look to stop traffic, he was the featured attraction in more ways than one. He was on every woman's radar screen including my mother. My mother and her girlfriends would swoon over him after a sighting and discuss how 'fine' he was. 'Fine' I'm sure he was. One thing led to another and he and my mother began dating in 1955.

Now I'm pretty certain that my father, a handsome singer at a popular nightclub, was not looking for a relationship that would culminate in the creation of a family. He could have any woman that he wanted. He was young and had plenty of time to choose. He was probably not even looking for a long-term relationship but only for a 'relationship'. This is probably where my parents' philosophies parted company. I am sure that even though my mother was not looking to start a family immediately, she was looking for a long-term, stable monogamous relationship. My father's interest in my mother, I believe meant one thing to him but something quite different to my mother.

I am sure my mother and other women were immediately seduced by his good looks, his charm, charisma, grace, and magnetic singing voice. Can you hear him? His lush, deep baritone voice was Billy Eckstine all the way. A black man, six feet tall, slender, honey-brown skin, soft straight dark brown hair, and way past easy on the eyes. Can you see him? Can you feel him?

My mom became pregnant with my sister in early 1955.

Certainly, during this era, and especially in the black working class, pregnancy without the benefit of marriage was unaccept-able. It did not fit the template. My mother knew that she could not announce to her family that she was pregnant out of wedlock. Even though my mother was the second youngest of eight chil-dren and my grandparents had tired and 'eased-up' a little in their parental activities, they were not going to be very happy about this event. You know how it happens; the early children get the opportunity to live by their parents' tougher standards while the later children benefit from their parents experience and sheer exhaustion and have an 'easier' time of it. However, unfortunately, pregnancy out of wedlock was a rule that stood as firm with the first child as it did with the last. Socially, it was a repugnant condition in which to find one-self, particularly if you were the pregnant party! My maternal grandparents had built a strong and upstanding reputation in their community and would have been shamed. My grandfather was a Deacon in the church and the family attended regularly.

By the mid to late 50's, my mother's six older brothers and sisters had already begun to build productive lives for themselves. Her two older brothers had taken over the family moving business, married, and started families of their own. Her youngest brother, who also worked in the family business, met a wonderful woman whom he married and moved to Cincinnati. Two of her sisters earned their undergraduate college degrees and began teaching. Another sister married and began a career in government service.

Shortly after my mother became pregnant at eighteen years of age, she announced their marriage and then the pregnancy. The order of the announcement was important. They lived with my mother's friend Shirley Allen and her husband during my mother's pregnancy, sharing a two-bedroom house on Seebalt Street, approximately six to eight blocks from Woodrow. It was a tumultuous relationship from the start. My father, a club singer in the evening, was out all hours of the night and not behaving like a husband or a prospective father. They fought both verbally and physically. Sometime after my sister was born, and my mother now nineteen, they moved to Indianapolis, Indiana so that my father could further pursue his singing career.

My father was 23 years of age when my sister was born and experiencing fatherhood for the second time. His first child, Charles Wright, Jr., was born in the mid 1950s in Chicago. His second child, Debra Wright, was born to my mother in January 1956 in Detroit. Exactly 355 days later, I was born in Indianapolis in January 1957.

Now there were two.

With my sister now just six months old, my mother was pregnant again with me. Now she was hundreds of miles away from home and unhappy. Again, the late hours, the drinking and women started in Indianapolis. Again, the fighting. Only six months into her pregnancy, I was born on January 12, 1957, 355 days after my sister.

My mother now twenty years old, had two children and a relationship that was falling apart. Shortly after my birth, they returned to Detroit and moved in with my father's family. The relationship continued to deteriorate and my mother moved back home to her parents, my grandfather, and Gammy.

It is here where my memories of childhood begin and where my father, the most important man in life, broke the chain and *let go of my hand.*

I did not get to pick the most important man in my life. The choice was not mine. I had no say in the selection of the man who would play such a significant role to shape and influence my life. I couldn't pick the man who would show me what it meant to be a father, a good father; a husband, a good husband; the man who would be grandfather my children; the man who would be my teacher, my role model, and my protector. I guess the world would be a perfect place if we could choose our parents. Instead, I got the man who would donate the biological component needed to produce life; sperm.

I got the man who would show me what it meant to be irresponsible, unloving; a poor example of a father and most of all a poor example of a man. I got a valuable lesson in life, however, I would not know how valuable until I became an adult.

Clearly, none of us has the opportunity to pick our parents. It is not the natural order of things. It's not God's plan. Suppose we could pick the most important man in our lives. Who would he be? What characteristics would be important? Surely, the ability to contribute sperm to the creation of life is a critical aspect of fatherhood, but for most men, this is an insignificant task. It drops to the bottom of the list of important characteristics.

The operative word here is 'choice'. The operative concept is 'choice'. Fathering a child and being a father are not synonymous. Sperm are a dime a dozen. Fathers have a responsibility to provide psychological, social, economic, educational and moral guidance to their children. Many fathers, even good fathers, are not capable or able to provide a perfect environment for their children but perfection is not what is important. There are countless fathers who couldn't begin to effectively articulate why they are good fathers or what made them good fathers. If asked by Regis Philbin on "Who Wants to be a Millionaire" what the most important factor to good fatherhood would be, the winning answer would be "love", because from love comes the willingness to put forth the effort to father. Good fathers do not have to be scholars, they need only to love their children and expend the effort to care for them and to be a parent. The result of this simple effort is priceless. Good fathers have to *choose* to be a link in the chain that creates the natural connection that should exist between parent and child.

Is my mother a culpable participant in this theatre? Yes. She made a poor decision, not once but twice. My father was plainly a poor choice. Unfortunately, she was drawn in by superficial characteristics and promises that he would live up to her expectations and care for her and his two children. He was not prepared to make such promises and ultimately walked away. My mother recognized her responsibility and role in where she stood. She routinely used the phrase "if you make your bed hard, you've got to sleep in it". She lived it and slept in it. She could have walked away also, but she 'chose' to love. She chose to stay. She held my hand.

My mother was a wonderful mother and responsible for the person I am today. Much of my inspiration comes from the difficulties she experienced and the fortitude she demonstrated in an effort not to succumb to those difficulties. My mother will always be with me and I am blessed that she was there for me. I am privileged that she cared enough to be strict, especially when I was a teenager to spare me from many potential pitfalls that an unsupervised environment could generate. My strength and fortitude come from my mother and her absence that began far too soon. I often think about how wonderful it would be to have her still with me and in the lives of my boys.

Webster defines parent as 'one that begets or brings forth offspring' and 'a person who brings up and cares for another. A parent is an entity from which one or more similar and separate things have developed, or to which they are attached, i.e., a natural connection. At the ends of these connections are our relatives who are extensions of this vision, linked, or joined together for the purpose of family'. My grandmother was the extended member of family who was also there for me. I will always love and cherish her. She did what she could to be the missing link in my life.

In situations where a marriage produces a child or children and the marriage does not survive, the links in the chain must not only survive but they must be fortified. While I believe that the institution of marriage is vital to the very fabric of 'family' and to our society, it is often not a permanent and unconditional union. Parenthood and fatherhood, however, are permanent and unconditional.

My father released himself of his responsibility for me and to me. He broke the chain.

He let go of my hand.

Chapter Five - Your Stone Rolled

"Blessed indeed is the man who hears many gentle voices call him father!"
— Lydia M. Child

I must have been ten years old when I realized that my father actually lived in the neighborhood. Prior to this, I would see him in and around the neighborhood, but never really gave much thought to where he lived. I just knew that he did not live with us. This revelation certainly explained the frequent sightings as we walked to the store or rode in my mother's car. Sometimes, we would see him driving a "paper bag" brown Chrysler or just walking down Tireman street.

I also realized at this same time that he had a wife; a person that he was married to that was not my mother. I wasn't quite sure how I felt about this, but I knew it perhaps explained why he wasn't with us. This aspect of his life played itself out as my sister and I visited a corner store two to three blocks from our home to buy penny candy. I believe the store was called "Helens". It was a small storefront with one large room where you could buy all of the typical things that are sold in a 'party store'. It was a microcosm of a grocery store. As children, we were only interested in the candy, chips, soda and popsicles and what could be bought with our allowance for doing chores. It was also an adventure of sorts to be able to walk to the corner store because it meant that we were 'free' to do what we wanted along the way and away from the oversight of my mother and grandmother.

We began to see my father working behind the counter with the woman who we eventually came to know as Helen, his wife. My initial instinct was to dislike Helen. Was she responsible for taking my father away? I later learned from my mother that Helen was also from the same neighborhood, but a few years older. One of the things I remember of her from my childhood was her big warm smile. She was always so pleasant when we came to the store giving us free candy and soda pop. She would introduce us to others in the store as 'Charlie's daughters'. She always made us feel special as she complemented our appearance and behavior. It did not take long for me to decide to like her.

My father was very warm and friendly as well. He too would also give us free candy and soda and call us his 'pretty girls'. He mesmerized me. He engulfed me with his good looks, his tall and handsome frame, and his deep and commanding voice. He really seemed to adore us in those few minutes. He always asked about my mother and the family. I was completely satisfied that he was the greatest father on earth, at that moment. What else could I ask for? I was his and he was mine. What other criteria did I need as a ten-year-old child who was looking to experience any opportunity to have a relationship with her father? Free from the burden of understanding what was really going on, I was accepting of what little I knew.

Helen and my mother established a connection at some point because Helen felt that my father should be more involved in our lives. I'm not sure how my mother really felt at the time, but she always spoke well of Helen. Helen contacted my mother and asked if my sister and I could spend the day at their house. I think my mother appreciated Helen's effort and genuinely liked her as a result. With my mother's approval, we visited their home with the intent to spend time with my father and to meet our brother and sister. This was a revelation for us. I can recall overhearing my mother talk about my father from another room where she mentioned other children, but it did not fully register that these children were brothers and sister or more appropri- ately, my half brother and sisters. I was a bit confused. Who were these 'others' and how did they come to be?

My mother dressed us in our one-piece blue and white outfits and off we went. Helen and my father lived in the neighborhood so we did not have far to travel. I don't recall many of the details of the afternoon, but two memories still stand tall in my mind.

The first was meeting my brother, Charles Jr. or "Charlie" as we called him. He was three to four years older and was abso- lutely gorgeous. He was a reincarnation of my father. He had wonderful black thick wavy hair, beautiful chestnut skin, and a million dollar smile. I can still remember him standing against the wall with his hands in his pockets and smiling brightly as we were introduced. At this stage in my life, I was just starting to notice boys and he was certainly one to notice! I had an instant crush! I learned that he lived in Chicago, which added a mystic that only enhanced my sisterly crush. I can remember thinking that he was sooooooooo cute and he was my bother.

I learned later from my mother that Charles Jr. was born in Chicago where he had lived with his mother Carla and his sister Vicky. Vicky was Carla's daughter from a previous relationship and was a few years older than Charlie. Charlie was in town for the summer living with my father's brother. Why he did not live with father and Helen for the summer, I'm not sure.

Finally, there was Trina. She was cute as well. She was this little high energy, high yellow girl, with two long braids, glasses, and missing teeth. She was so sweet and so much fun. I believe she was seven or eight at the time. Trina lived on the west side of Detroit within walking distance from my home and on the same block as my father's brother. Because she lived so close to our uncle, Trina had an opportunity as a child to see my father quite often. Her relationship with him was probably the most unique among all of his children with whom he did not live.

I can recall that pictures were taken to capture the fun and excitement of the day. The afternoon ended with promises that we would get together soon, however it would never happen again but it is imprinted in my mind forever.

Years later, Helen would give me a precious gift of multiple family pictures. One picture in particular, I will treasure forever. It is the only picture that I have with my father. These pictures tell a story that I had not known. They speak to me loudly of my history, my past and my legacy. For the first time, I can look into the faces of my grandparents and see myself.

Now there were four.

Chapter Six – And Rolled, and Rolled, and Rolled

"The most important thing a father can do for this children is to love their mother." — Theodore M. Hersburgh, President, Notre Dame

Several months after our summer visit with my father and Helen, Helen gave birth to Kenya in January 1969. We heard about the birth from kids in the neighborhood.

Now there were five.

We had very few occasions to see Kenya because we never visited my father and Helen again. We watched Kenya grow up though a series of calendars that Helen would publish yearly with Kenya featured along with other members of her family. She was a striking child who grew into a beautiful and smart woman. I can remember thinking how lucky Kenya was to be featured on these calendars. It gave her sort of a movie star quality in my young mind.

My father and Helen opened a commercial printing business on Livernois called C & H Printing. My father had grown up in the printing business, learning his craft from his father and brothers. I can recall driving by the shop in my mother's car and looking in to see if I could catch a glimpse of him. Of course, I never saw him, but it did not stop me from looking every time. Ultimately, Helen and my father divorced and Helen maintained the print shop. She is an outstanding businesswoman today; still operating the shop later renamed E & H Printing.

Throughout our teenage years, my sister and I saw my father occasionally on the street. All of these sightings were chance encounters. We would see him on a city bus as we were on our way to Cass Technical High School in downtown Detroit or we would see him on the street as we rode the city bus to get to my grandmother's house after school. We would see him drive down my grandmother's street in his car, however he would never stop to say hello. I suspect that to stop and say hello would invite a chilly to hostile response from my mother. My mother fought with my father throughout our childhood to receive financial assistance or child support. She never got a dime as she pursued him on her own because he simply did not want to pay. When my mother decided to pursue him through the legal system, she encountered extreme difficulty because he often worked in venues where he reported little or no income. In other words, he was paid under the table! With no reportable income, the 'Friend of the Court', the Michigan division of the circuit court system charged with enforcing child support activities, had no tangible resources to pursue.

In 1969, my mother married my stepfather, Kenneth. We moved to the northwest side of the city to Mendota Street. In the spring of 1972 or 1973, my sister and I were getting off the Fenkell bus to go home after leaving Cass Technical High School for the day. We normally, got off the bus at Birwood & Fenkell and walked home from there. On this day, as we got off the bus, we saw my father enter a building near the bus stop. We called out to him and he stopped and flashed that big smile. He waited as we ran to meet him and hugged us both and invited us into the building where he was opening a new printing business.

I can remember feeling very uncomfortable because we were somewhere that we did not have permission to be. My mother would have been way past angry. We were taught to be careful and to never get into anyone's car, even if we knew the person and certainly never to go into someone's home or building, as in this case with my father, without her knowledge. We were so excited to see him that all of the rules, so innate and instinctive, suddenly did not exist.

My sister as usual took the lead and we followed my father into the building. We stood in the front office area and he asked us the usual questions and made the usual comments about how we were growing up so fast. After a few minutes, I was getting a little nervous because we were already ten minutes late getting home. I was very keenly aware of my mother's rules and took exceptional care not to violate them. The punishment was never worth the benefit of the crime. I urged my sister to hurry along. We talked for a few minutes and exchanged phone numbers.

Debra and I were particularly excited to give our phone number because we had several months earlier in January, been given our own phone line as a birthday present. Debra wrote her name and our phone number on the back of one of his business cards. He placed the card in his pocket, gave us a hug and we hurried home. We decided to run most of the way to make up for some of the time we spent with my father. My mother expected us home at a certain time and being late was not an option!

We were so excited to see my father. It had been quite some time since our last encounter with him. He was charming and friendly as always and promised to call. He assured us that we could stop by the print shop anytime.

When we arrived home, we told my mother we saw my father as we got off the bus, but we left out the part where we went into the print shop. We of course reported the meeting with my father with some degree of excitement. She of course did not share our enthusiasm. She was very curious about the location of the shop, but not much else. She did say that if we saw him again, she did not want us to go inside of the shop! We looked at one another and shook our heads up and down to indicate that we understood the instruction. We immediately went to our room and chuckled as we discussed our decision to leave out the part where we entered the shop with my father! We would surely have been on punishment at that very moment had she known. We chattered on about my father and our hope that he would call. I think we believed that he would call.

Several days after the visit with my father, the phone rang in our bedroom and I answered.

The female voice on the end said "Debra?"

"No", I said. "She's not here right now. Can I give her a message?"

She said, "Who are you"? in a very angry tone. I could tell that she was not one of our friends. She clearly sounded much older.

"This is Robin. Who is this?"

"I found the name Debra and this phone number on the back of Charles Wrights' business card and I want to know how you know him?"

I was immediately intimidated as her voice and tone escalated. I was only fifteen years old, but I knew enough to sense that this was not going to be pleasant. I remembered that Debra had written her name and phone number on the back of one of my father's business cards when we saw him a few days earlier. Who could this be and why was she so angry? She obviously thought 'Debra' was a woman my father met and exchanged phone numbers with.

Afraid to answer, I said timidly, "Charles Wright is my father. My sister Debra and I saw him last week and we gave him our phone number".

Maybe this information would calm her down if she knew we were his daughters. She would surely know then that she was making a mistake.

She returned fire saying "Your father? You don't know that! Who is your mother?"

What did she mean by that?, I thought.

"My mother is Luvenia"

What would she say next? I sat down on the bed as if to steady myself as the conversation was moving to an uncomfortable place.

"You don't know that he's our father. He was never married to your mother so how do you know that he's really your father?" she said, her voice lowering to an angry growl.

What did she say?, I thought. Of course, my mother and father were married, weren't they?

I felt like my head was spinning! I will remember the conversation for the rest of my life. I was instantly confused. I had never considered that my parents had never been married. Was she telling the truth? I did not know this person on the phone, yet she was telling me things about my life and about my mother. It was an information overload at fifteen years old. It was cruel.

"I don't know what you're talking about!" I replied as my eyes began to tear. "He *is* my father", I shouted!

She hung up.

Stunned, I sat down on the side of the bed and cried very

quietly. At the age of fifteen, I knew what this meant, if it was in fact true. It meant that my sister and I were conceived out of wedlock and were illegitimate children. While I was not sure what this really meant from a social perspective, I understood it enough to know that it was not good. I understood that my mother wanted desperately to prevent my sister or me from becoming pregnant before we married. Could this be why?

I contemplated what to do next. I had to tell my mother. I was afraid because I knew that telling her would summon a level of anger and emotion that I didn't want to be a part of even though I knew that she would not be angry with me. Just then, my sister came in and I told her what happened. She was shocked as well. Debra agreed; my mother had to know.

My sister and I slowly crept downstairs where my mother was preparing dinner. I was petrified to tell her but I knew that I had to do it. I told her I had something to tell her. The look on her face was one of sheer terror. We moved from the kitchen to the dining room table. After a few moments of silence, I finally told her of the phone call and held my breath for her reaction. She was horrified! She immediately clasped her face with both hands and began to cry. This could only mean one thing. The information or some part of the information was true.

When she gathered herself she wanted to know about the caller, but I could not tell her. "Who was it?" she demanded.

"Mommy, I don't know!" I exclaimed. "She didn't say her name and she hung up!"

She immediately went into her bedroom and returned with a phone book. She rushed to the phone and dialed a number. She hung up very quickly; the number was no longer connected. She placed another call and got the same result. She was getting angry now and slammed the receiver into the cradle. She was trying to call my father.

Just then, we heard the side door open and in walked my stepfather, Kenneth. He could tell by the look on our faces that something was wrong. We sat quietly while my mother told him what had occurred. He could see the anger in my mother and the hurt on our faces. He politely asked my sister and I to go upstairs until dinner was ready. We did as he asked very quickly because we really wanted to get out of there!

"What do you think she's going to do?" I said to Debra as we sat on the side of our beds facing each another. She shrugged her shoulders to indicate that she did not know. We turned on the television and quietly waited for dinner because we knew there would be more to come.

My mother called us to dinner an hour later. When we arrived at the table, it was completely set with plates, salad bowls, silverware and condiments, as it was always. We sat down as a family to have dinner in this way each day. It was a nice time to just sit and talk and interact with one another without the television and other interruptions. It was also a great time for my mother to lay down her rules and expectations.

Today the conversation would be different. We listened as

my mother proceeded to tell us that she and my father were in fact never married. He could not marry her because he had been married to Carla in Chicago and was not divorced. She explained that my father had separated from Carla and was pursuing a divorce when she became pregnant with my sister Debra. She assured us that she loved us and would always love us. She did not want us to feel insecure or flawed because we were born out of wedlock.

My mother went on to explain that they both led their parents to believe that they were married because it was unacceptable to be pregnant and unmarried in 1955. They would have brought significant shame on their parents and family if my mother had given birth out of wedlock.

I can imagine that it was a traumatic time for her. She had obviously engaged in a relationship with a man who was married and was now pregnant. She was faced with constructing an untruth that would protect her and my father from further scrutiny.

We were very upset that evening, but not just for ourselves. We could see the pain, anger and shame that my mother felt as she talked with us. Most profound were her feelings of embarrassment. She was forced by the mean spirit of another person to disclose something that she did not want to tell. My mother was always in control where we were concerned, however on that day she did not have control. Someone, a woman associated with my father, had decided to impose her cruelty upon a child. This someone obviously knew enough about my father and his history to impart information that was factual. This someone, apparently, feeling threatened, was heartless in her pursuit of my father imposing pain upon my mother, and my sister and me. My mother had long ago moved on with her life and we had managed our lives quite well without my father. Whatever her relationship was with my father, the caller certainly had no reason to feel threatened. Her cruelty was simply unwarranted and gratuitous.

The day's revelation left a chill on a hot summer day, changing the chemistry of our family and creating more questions than answers. I knew that we would not hear much more about the phone call because it was such an uncomfortable discussion for my mother. I did, in the days to come hear my mother on the phone talking to her sisters and her girlfriends. She was determined to get to the bottom of it and find out who made the call. The topic, however, was never discussed with us again.

I can honestly say that I did feel ashamed that I was born out of wedlock. As a young teenager, I was very impressed and interested in pop music. I often took the time to memorize study and understand the lyrics to a song that I enjoyed. One such song that became a favorite and very relevant to my life was 'Love Child" by Diana Ross and the Supremes. The song released in late 1968 was notable for its then controversial subject matter of illegitimacy. The lyrics spoke to my feelings of shame because my father too left and 'never married mama' leaving me with the feeling that I had no name. I think this is in part, the reason why I hyphenate my maiden name and my married name. I have always wanted to hang on to my father's name, Wright.

In 1973, my father married Edna. To their union another beautiful child, Karen Wright, was born. We only saw Karen a few times as she grew up. I recall seeing her at my aunt's retirement party when she was perhaps six or seven years of age. She was so cute, with dark brown skin, long hair, and big beautiful smile. I would not see her again until my father's death.

Now there were six.

My mother always told me I would come to know my father for myself when I became an adult. It did not take long. My sister Debra married in 1980 and decided that she wanted my father to walk her down the isle. This decision created significant controversy with my mother because she felt that my father was undeserving of this special honor. She was furious, but because my sister paid for the most of the wedding, she really did not have much of a voice.

My sister proceeded with her plans to have my father to participate in the wedding and he agreed to do so. We were all very apprehensive, because my father had proven himself so unreliable. Unfortunately, when my sister tried to reach him to participate in the rehearsals, he could not be found. When she did locate him, he was drunk and incoherent. This was surely a sign that perhaps he could not be relied upon to show up on the day of the wedding. She was so disappointed. She was also embarrassed because my mother was certainly able to say, "I told you so!"

My sister's desire to have my father participate in her wedding can be explained by an article featured in 'Today's Father Magazine'. The writer discusses a research study, conducted by a doctoral student who looked at the bereavement patterns of twenty adolescent girls whose fathers had recently died. The question the researcher asked was what they would miss the most about losing their fathers. One answer showed up repeatedly among the twenty girls. Most of the girls deeply regretted the fact that their father would not be there to walk them down the aisle when they got married. Even though my father was living, his significant absence was a loss similar to that of a father dying. I believe my sister wanted very much to experience that golden moment reserved only for a father and daughter.

What is interesting about a father walking his daughter down the aisle is its true meaning; a father 'giving his daughter away'. The ritual speaks to the bond between father and daughter and the process to sever that bond. In the ceremony, the father takes his daughter by the hand and leads her up to her soon-to-be husband awaiting her at the alter. He transfers her hand to the man whose name she will assume. Having a father give his daughter away is also a very loving moment between a father and daughter because her hand transfers from the very first man that loved her to the man with whom she will spend the rest of her life.

My father was not deserving of this honor because there was

no bond established with his daughter so there was none to sever. He was certainly her father, but not the first man to love her.

Disappointment again.

In the summer of 1986, my cousin invited my boys and I to attend her daughter's first birthday party. My oldest son, Ricky, four years old at the time was very excited. My half sister Trina was there with her son as were many other family members. It was really a fun opportunity to mix and mingle with the side of my family that I saw so rarely.

To my surprise, my father arrived about halfway through the party. I had not anticipated that he would attend, but I was pleased that he had come. I climbed the stairs from the basement and greeted him with a hug. As I released him from my embrace, I saw a woman around my age, standing next to him who was very pregnant. He turned and touched her arm and introduced her as his friend. At that moment, my mind filled with many thoughts. It was a turning point. This woman was not his wife! Was he still married? I later learned he was no longer with his wife and daughter, however he was not divorced. He was having another child.

My father had six children and was now fifty-two years of age. To my knowledge, he had not taken care of my sister and me in any way. He never visited, he never called, and he never participated in our lives. I assumed the same or similar scenario played out in the lives of my four half brothers and sisters. What was going on? I sat and watched him during the birthday party as if I was going to find the answer on his face, in his behavior, or somewhere in the room. What was wrong with this man? Not only was he still married but he was clearly bold enough to bring the new relationship and the evidence thereof to a family event. My morals and values would not have allowed me to do that! No one, however, seemed surprised by it all because I am sure it was not the first time they were witnesses to this kind of behavior.

My Dad went on to have three more beautiful children, Charles Wright, III, Jeanette Wright, and Creighton Wright.

Now there were nine. Count with me, one, two, three, four, five, six, seven, eight, and NINE.

Nine children with six different women.

Nine.

Chapter Seven – I Celebrate Your Life …

"Where there is no struggle, there is no strength."
— Oprah Winfrey

The day of my father's funeral proved to be a more rousing and emotional, experience than I could ever have imagined. My sister Debra had flown in from Minneapolis to attend the funeral.

The funeral was held at Hartford Memorial Baptist church, one of the largest and most elite black churches in the city. The church was very crowded as expected, full of friends and family. As I entered, the feelings that I had pushed aside in the days since his death, were reappearing. My sister and I could hear the whispers of those who pointed us out as 'two of his children' as we approached the casket.

As I viewed my father's body, I felt a great sense of loss and a swell of sadness. Here lying before me was the man whose biology I contained within my body. He was not there for my entire life, and would now never be there. For the last time, I would study his handsome face, ravished by age and illness, his beautiful hair, grayed but in place and his features that were my features, the shape of his face, his eyes, his nose, his lips and the color of his skin, shadowed by death. I looked down at his hands and saw the familiar injury to his finger that he suffered years earlier in a printing press. I saw on his face, a life made difficult by poor choices, alcohol, and tobacco. He looked sad as if he was sorry for the hurt that he had inflicted upon others.

When we reached to our seats, we began to read the obituary and saw that even in death, he seemed to elude responsibility for the way in which he lived his life. His obituary, the final written document intended to offer a brief biography of his life, was written to exclude three very important facts about his life. His obituary excluded three beautiful children born out of a relation-ship that took place outside of his marriage to Edna. Charles, III, Jeannette, and Creighton were not listed as offspring on the obituary. While I hurt for them, I could only imagine the hurt and pain that his wife endured in what she surely tried to make a good marriage. I am sure that she wanted what most women want from a marriage, a committed and loving husband. She undoubtedly worked hard and made many sacrifices to be a good wife and mother as evidenced by her beautiful daughter Karen. She perhaps didn't get what she was looking for but she was not alone. Most of the women in my father's life got promises, disappointments, and children to raise alone.

On this day, three young, innocent, and impressionable children were simply erased as if they did not exist.

My father was clearly loved by his family. The baby, he was not expected to leave this earth before his older sisters and brothers. The severity of his illness and subsequent death had come as a shock to everyone. The emotion displayed as the funeral director prepared to close the casket was so rousing that there was not a dry eye in the church. Loved ones were screaming and crying in a way that surprised me. I knew so little of his relationships with family members that I had not contemplated the significant show of emotion.

As the funeral proceeded, several of my cousins who spoke to express their feelings about my father further struck me. I was stunned to learn that he had taught some of them to drive, that he had taken them to events and loved to play and have fun with them. They really loved "Uncle Charlie". They shared memories and experiences that my father could have created with me! I could have grieved these memories, but that honor was bestowed on someone else who was not his daughter. I felt a wave of anger and jealously. I had no such memories to savor or to replay in my mind. They had something precious that I did not have. They had memories. I cried because I felt pushed aside and forgotten again. For a moment, I made my father's death about me.

My father apparently did have the capacity to love and to be at least an uncle if he could not be a father. Maybe, that was the key. As an uncle, he bore no real *responsibility* for his nieces and nephews. He could be the fun uncle and walk away and he was good at walking away.

After the funeral and burial, everyone returned to the church for a repast. I sat down across the table from one of my aunts who I had not seen in quite some time. She was related to me as an aunt through marriage to my father's brother. As we ate and talked, she commented on how much I looked like my father and how beautiful she thought my hair was styled.

She then came completely out of left field and said "…but you seem awfully uppity".

I was not having a good day already. I thought for a moment that I did not hear her correctly.

"Excuse me. What did you say?"

"I said you seem awfully uppity"

"Why would you say that?" I questioned.

"Because you seem to have your nose in the air"

I was stunned. You could hear a pin drop at the table. I didn't know what to say or how to respond. My instinct was to tell her she was being rude, in a nice way, of course. She was my elder and my aunt. I chose to take the high road.

"Excuse me. I need to go to the ladies room". I left the table and went to the hallway to cry. My sister Debra and Kenya joined me.

As the family gathered at my aunt's home after the church dinner, many offered their condolences to my siblings and me. Everybody was very kind and had very wonderful stories to tell about my father and the experiences that they shared with him. A family friend spoke about my father growing up and his outstanding singing voice. Someone else talked about what a talented printer he was. These were all interesting and cherished insights because we knew so little about my father.

An aunt, who lived out of state, began to talk with Debra and me, commenting that it was so wonderful to see all of Charlie's children together.

"It is really so nice to see all of you guys at one time", she said. "You are all such beautiful kids and you all look so much alike. You all look like Charlie".

We smiled because she was right. We all had the "Wright" look. As I looked around the room, I noted several physical characteristics that many of us shared; our caramel skin tone, dark soft hair and slender build.

She then leaned into us and said one tone above a whisper, "It's too bad Cecelia is not here. She is the only one who is missing."

I immediately turned to look at her.

"Who is Cecelia?"

She stared back at us, as stunned as we were because it was clear that we had no knowledge of Cecelia.

"You don't know about Cecelia?"

We could guess what was coming. *'She's the only one who is missing'* could only mean one thing. Wow! Debra and I had no idea! There was silence. The stunned looks on our faces answered the question.

"You didn't know?" she said again. Still stunned, we did not answer. We could not. She looked perplexed. The cat was out of the bag and she couldn't put it back in. She did not stall for too long because she knew she couldn't get that cat back in the bag! She probably assumed that we knew because after all, we were no longer children. We were thirty-nine and forty years of age.

"A half sister? We have another half sister?" I said. "How could that be? "I said. I immediately thought what a dumb statement! I knew exactly how that could happen. My sister turned and looked at me as if to say 'what are you thirty-nine going on four?'

As with many life-changing events, time dissolves the impact. It is the 'plop-plop-fiz-fiz' theory in that Cecelia's mere existence caused a significant degree of angst and relief. Angst not because of Cecelia personally, because of course I knew nothing about her other than the fact that she existed. Angst because she was now the tenth child, and for me the eighth half-sibling. Relief, because I now knew something that I should have know before. This was already soap opera material! Were there more children? Did I have other half brothers and sisters? I wanted to know more about her, but my aunt had lost contact with her and her mother many years ago. My aunt went on to tell us that Cecelia had lived with her for a brief period during her childhood.

I often wonder if I've passed Cecelia on the street and even found myself looking twice at women whom I resemble. Is she still living? Does she have children of her own? She and I would be very close in age, perhaps only months apart. My aunt described the early life that she knew about as 'difficult', suggesting that her mother's life was troubled.

Unbelievable.

Now there were ten. TEN!

But maybe not. Rumor has it that there are children in Bermuda.

Chapter Eight - ... and Cry No More

"It hurts to love someone and not be loved in return, but what is more painful is to love someone and never find the courage to let that person know how you feel." — Unknown Author

Dear Daddy,

I still cry when I think about how you could walk away from me so easily. I will be 50 years old in 2007 and the pain is as acute today as it was 30 years ago. It is unthinkable to some that I could still feel this way after so many years. I have no explanation for those who think that the time erases the pain. I do know that your absence has created an indelible impression on my heart and soul that will always be there.

Perhaps, you did not understand how significant a father is to the life of his daughter. Perhaps, you did not know that fathers are the template in the lives of their daughters that they will use to select a spouse or significant other. Maybe, you didn't under-stand that it was your responsibility to listen, postulate, and guide my thoughts and attitudes about boys and relationships. Only you could have done this. Only you. Perhaps, you did not know that daughters need that 'male' strength, security, and direction that only a father can provide. Perhaps, you had better things to do. Perhaps, you were not capable. Perhaps.

Dad, when you were free to run and do as you pleased, I wondered where you were. When I took my first step, you were not there. I was too young to know that I would "walk through" my life without you. By the time I had grown into a 'big girl' just like Debra, and started kindergarten, you had fathered two additional children who would also walk through life without you.

At five years of age, a brick carelessly thrown by a neighbor-hood child injured me. I got fifteen stitches, but you were not there. I can remember being so frightened and clinging to my mother. I got my tonsils removed and ate ice cream to sooth my pain. You were not there. I rode a two-wheel bike for the first time all by myself. My mother was there. I sang "Up, Up and Away" at the Sampson Elementary Talent Show and you where not there to be proud of me. You were not there, yet you lived ten to fifteen minutes away. I went on my first date when I was sixteen. You were not there. You taught your nieces to drive but you were not there to teach me to drive. I graduated from Cass Technical High School in 1975 and you were not there. You did not call. You did not send a card. When I met the man that I would marry, you were absent. You were nowhere to be found. When I married, you did not walk me down the aisle because there was no bond between us. When I graduated from college, you were not there.

When my sons were born, you were creating three more lives that you would ultimately not father. Giving birth to them, I felt an innate and unconditional love that a parent should feel for their child, whether mother or father. I can remember holding each of them for the first time and feeling completely overwhelmed with emotion. Today, they are wonderful young men who know and understand family. They experienced the benefit of having both a mother and a father in their lives. They will be good fathers should they 'chose' to father children because they have both been the product of good and responsible parenting. As odd as it is to say, I 'introduced' you to your grandsons. You didn't even know their names.

My mother died of breast cancer in 1990. Again, you were not there. You called to offer your condolences, but I could hear the intoxication in your voice. I grieved for the loss of my mother and could not understand why God would take her from me. I honestly wondered why he would take her and not you. She was such a vital part of my life and to those who loved her. She contributed to the world in a loving and giving way. She was the best mother that she could be as demonstrated by raising three children without their fathers to become productive and sustainable adults. I am proud to say that she is the reason why my sister, brother and I all have a formal education and the intellectual and emotional tools necessary to support our families and ourselves. I am proud to call her mother.

Unfortunately my words and thoughts are sometimes harsh, because I did not know you. I recently learned that you were a Marine, that you were interested and involved in politics. I just didn't know you.

Writing this book has been a cathartic experience for me. I can now understand why I felt the immediate sense of panic when I got the phone call that you were very ill and hospitalized. I was aware that you had been hospitalized before; however, I was not made aware at the time. Each of the previous occurrences had apparently not been as serious as this one. I knew that you were in trouble this time. It was at this moment that I knew that I loved you. You are my father and I am a product of you. I exist in part because of you. I realize that perhaps that link or connection between us had not been irrevocably broken, as I had once concluded because there is an aspect of our connection that does create an unconditional bond. That unconditional 'condition' is more than DNA. It is a 'father-daughter' covenant; a formal, solemn, and binding agreement achieved through the natural and genetic process of life creation. This covenant is held in an ever so unique place in the hollow of both of our souls.

Dad, in this very small, but wonderful place, I can imagine that you loved me at the moment that I was conceived. As I grew from an embryo to form my tiny brain, my very being was aware that you were there. With every beat of my new heart, I felt your love pulsate through my veins, nourishing my body and mind with your kindness, your warmth, and your spirit. As my limbs took form, I felt you take my hand and promise to be my life guide and my hero. I knew that you would be there always to walk with me as life challenged and rewarded me. As my senses developed, I could hear your voice over the roar of the embryonic fluid, and I knew of your commanding voice, your intellect, and your zeal and passion for life.

In this very small place, I saw your smile and was soothed because I knew that I would see that smile for the rest of your life. I was comforted knowing that your eyes, as they met mine for the first time, were filled with adoration and hope for my life. As you held me in your arms, we finalized and executed our covenant. It was done.

In that very small place, you loved me and I loved you. Life did not penetrate the walls of our space. Life was left outside with all of its expectations and disappointments. Reality did not penetrate our space. In that little space, we could just be.

By instinct, I would protect this place from harm because it was all I had of you that offered true meaning. The memories I held were so minute when measured over a lifetime or even just my childhood. I saw you just as often in my adult life as I did as a child. There were surely times when I did see you, but those memories were fading as I approached 50 years of age.

Today, most of my memories of you are pleasant because they include the 'starry-eyed' experiences seen through the eyes of a child. Into young adulthood, my memories are not quite so pleasant because it is then that I began to understand the roles and responsibilities that exist in personal relationships, particularly as they apply to one's children. My mother was there. That is clear. My mother loved my sister and me. That is clear. You were not there. That is very clear. However, in order to love you, I know that I must remember my vision of the world as a 'starry-eyed' child with a big imagination. It is such a sweet spot. It is such an easy place to be. It is a place that gives me the freedom to forget what I want to forget and to imagine you in any way that I wish. I often see young children and a father in the mall, in the park, or in a restaurant, and I say a silent prayer that that father is always in his child's life and the child is someday aware and appreciative of his or her father's critical role.

Father-daughter relationships are so unique that stepfathers and alternate father figures, regardless to how outstanding the effort, are not able to fill the void of a father absent by choice. The 'choiceful' component of the relationship is what is so disturbing because it is rejection. Who wants to be rejected, especially by a father? How hurtful is that? Even if there is an outstanding stepfather in the picture, there is still that little secret place that wants to know and imagines that their real father is there.

I will protect this little place because I need it so very much. I want to love you. I have always wanted to love you, but it has never been without effort. I live a paradigm that says a father must love his daughter. It is a part of the natural order of things. No weapons formed against my special place shall prosper because even more important than me loving you, I need you to love me. I need to feel that you loved me as you lived on this earth and still love me as you sleep never to awaken.

With this special place in tact, I do understand that in reality, I could not get from you what you could not give. You did not have the capacity to be a father and to care and love your children. You could not love me. You were not capable. I am ok with this reality, because I have my make-believe place that I will covet and protect.

Dad, I now understand that perhaps you did make the best decision for all of us to leave our lives. You were not prepared to father children even though you produced them at a record level. My life would have been substantially different had my mother not been strong enough to move forward with her life without you. As I look at what little of your life I know about, I am able to see behaviors that would not have been conducive to family life. I am glad that you were not there to puncture our lives with dysfunction. Although I still cry for the experiences that I believe I deserved to have with you, I am glad that you removed yourself from us.

I am glad Dad that you chose my mother. She stepped up to the plate and hit a homerun. She carried us with love from base to base, leading and guiding our lives like a ship on a midnight sea. She rounded each base making sure that we absorbed and retained all of the knowledge and tools that we would need to sustain our lives because she would not always be there. She headed into home base with her children ahead of her because she always put us first. She ran those bases without you. She supported us without you. She was an outstanding mother and I will pay tribute to her for the rest of my life by pursuing my role as a parent and mother with all that I have. She lived by example, the true meaning of Mother.

Dad, you cheated yourself out of a wonderful and fulfilling kinship with my sister and me. You allowed yourself to be misled in thinking that the life you chose was more rewarding than nurturing, guiding, and having a presence in the lives of your children. You missed what you can never get back. I know first hand what you will never know. I have experienced and continue to experience what you missed with my children. I know that I am a better parent because you helped me to see the painful impact of absence.

I know the old Chinese proverb "A child's life is like a piece of paper on which every person leaves a mark" is true. You left a mark on my life even in your absence. For many years, I danced around this mark, choosing to see it and feel it as pain. I now choose not to see it as blemish, but to color it in with the lively hues of life. I am rewriting my script and painting over those pain marks so that I can see my life through the lenses that God and my mother intended for me to see.

Finally, Dad, I am setting you free from your obligation to me because I know that holding on to the resentment that I have held for so long is what keeps me a victim. I want to stop the hurt. I choose not to hurt. I didn't get to choose the man who would be my father, but I can choose to forgive. I choose to forgive you. I can now wish you a peaceful eternal sleep with a purer heart and mind. I forgive you. I will cry no more.

Harriet Beecher Stowe once said, "The bitterest tears shed over graves are for words left unsaid and deeds left undone". I have spoken and my deed is done.

Your Daughter,

Robin

About the Author

Robin Wright King is an entrepreneur, author and lecturer, living in Lathrup Village, Michigan. Raised in Detroit, she attended Detroit Public Schools, graduated from Wayne State University with a BS degree in Business Administration and an MBA in Finance from the University of Detroit.

Through her own experience, Robin Wright King highlights a catastrophic social and cultural issue plaguing the African American community: *fatherless daughters.* Her journey to fatherlessness began with the move to Detroit, at one year of age, as her parents ended their relationship, leaving her mother with the sole responsibility to raise her, and her sister Debra.

Growing up without her father, who lived often within a five to ten mile radius, she longed to have the typical 'father-daughter' relationship. Her father chose, however, to have no involvement in her life, never sending a birthday card, never a phone call to say hello and never a visit to see that she was ok. Reaching adulthood, she continued to be troubled by her father's absence and began to study the fatherlessness crisis in the United States. Of particular interest was the impact that fatherlessness has on African American females. She found a substantial amount of information that studied the impact of fatherlessness for boys in general as well as African American boys, but very little with regard to girls and almost nothing for African American girls.

Wright King, married and the mother of two sons Roderick and Ryan Brown, has experienced parenthood first hand and learned the true meaning of unconditional love and the critical role that both parents play in raising a child.

Her first book, entitled *Papa Was a Rolling Stone: A Daughter's Journey to Forgiveness* (2006), details her life and very personal experience with fatherlessness. It speaks to the crisis that threatens to change the fabric of the traditional family structure, particularly for African Americans and the need for young men and women to be more discerning in their sexual behaviors and choices to mitigate the impact of fatherlessness.

Wright King is married to Rev. Dr. Oscar King, III and is involved in her church where she conducts a series of financial education seminars and other programs designed to empower adults and youth. She is launching a program called "Fathers First" to promote the involvement of fathers in the lives of their children.

Contact Wright King for lecture or speaking engagements at *www.robinwrightking.com.*

Resources

i. Odum, Charles, "Cosby Challenges Spelman Graduates 'to take charge'", Ledger-Enquirer.com, May 14, 2006, Associated Press

ii. Bankole Thompson, "Fathers need jobs, not jail", The Michigan Citizen, May 2005

iii. Ibid

iv. Vivian M. Baulch and Patricia Zacharias, "Detroit Giant Stove and Tire", *The Detroit News,* The "World's Largest Stove" debuted at the 1893 World's Columbian Exposition in Chicago and was moved in 1926 up Jefferson to the west side of the approach to the Belle Isle Bridge.

v. B. Carlisle / R. Thomas, "Butterfly Kisses", © 1997 Diadem Music Publishing / Polygram Int'l Music Publishing

vi. Michelle Ingrassia, "Endangered Family", *Newsweek Magazine*, August 30, 1993, Reported by Farai Chideya, Michelle

Ingrassia, Vern E. Smith and Pat Wingert

vii. Ibid

viii. "Births to Teenagers in the United States, 1940-2000," National Vital Statistics Reports (Hyattsville, MD: National Center for Health Statistics, 2001), S. J. Ventura, T. J. Mathews, and B. E. Hamilton, September 25, vol. 49, no.10, p. 4., references, 17, 18, 19, 28, 36, 37, & 38

ix. "Births to Teenagers in the United States, 1940-2000," National Vital Statistics Reports (Hyattsville, MD: National Center for Health Statistics, 2001), S. J. Ventura, T. J. Mathews, and B. E. Hamilton, September 25, vol. 49, no.10, references, 73, 74 & 75

x. "Teen pregnancy more likely for fatherless girls", Sydney Morning Herald National, Bettina Arndt, September 23, 2003

xi. "Footprints", Margaret Fishback Powers, 1964

xii. Joy Jones, "Marriage Is for White People", The Washington Post Company, March 26, 2006; B01

xiii. "A Father's Heart for Daughters", Today's Father Magazine, fatherhood.miningco.com